Take Heart YZ: The Sequel
2018 published by Gospel App Ministries

Copyright 2018 William H. Senyard
No part of this book may be reproduced in any manner without prior written permission from the publisher.

ISBN-10: 0-9975461-3-1

ISBN-13: 978-0-9975461-3-2

All Scripture quotations, unless otherwise stated, are from the Holy Bible: New International Version (NIV). Copyright 1973, 1978, 1984 by International Bible Society.

Acknowledgements

I remain deeply grateful for my wife Eunice, my board, family and friends who have captured the vision of resetting the Church of Jesus Christ back to the simple uncluttered Gospel.

May God bless it to His glory and use it for many new experiences of the stunning abundant life purchased 2000 years ago by Jesus alone for all who participate in His calling and Spirit.

I want to give a special shout out to my brilliant, talented and humble songwriter daughter, Allie, for her inspiring song, "Take Heart." Also I am indebted to Allie, my son John, as well as newcomer Elise Farinelli for their wonderful work as THYZ spokespersons. It is so easy to work with such a talented team.

Special thanks to Jeff and Aubrey Buster, Howie and Lanay James, Jim and Pam Horner, John Armstrong, Eric Protzman, as well as Scott and Joannie Barth for all of their love, encouragement and support.

"I have told you these things, so that in me you may have peace. In this world you will have trouble. But take heart! I have overcome the world."
John 16:33 NIV

Take heart

Contents

Welcome and Instructions	vii
Module #0: Review of the Gospel App Shape	ix
Module #1: Miraculous Faith	1
Module #2: The Simple Uncluttered Gospel	15
Module #3: Miraculous Relationships	29
Module #4: Miraculous Forgiveness	39
Module #5: Miraculous Repentance	53
Module #6: Miraculous Prayer	65
Module #7: Miraculous Evangelism	75
Preaching the Gospel to Myself Review	85
Partial Bibliography	89

Take heart

Welcome and Instructions

"Teaching Christians how to receive and apply the singular Gospel of Christ to the real lives of real people in the real world--beginning with me!"

Welcome Jesus-follower to Take Heart: The Sequel. Since you are reading this, you already have a workbook. You will also need to access the videos that correspond to each module. They are listed below. For your convenience, we are providing web links in both Hi-Def and Standard-Definition. Enjoy. You may watch them as many times as you would like. Take heart, child of God.

Hi-Definition Video Links

Module 0: https://rebrand.ly/3xi1aje

Module 1: https://rebrand.ly/sobcrrz

Module 2: https://rebrand.ly/kb2my03

Module 3: https://rebrand.ly/qmf926b

Module 4: https://rebrand.ly/etd9pcf

Module 5: https://rebrand.ly/2tl8q16

Module 6: https://rebrand.ly/zdpx3ui

Module 7: https://rebrand.ly/fe2r3lt

Standard-Definition Video Links

Module 0: https://rebrand.ly/rof1rey

Module 1: https://rebrand.ly/6zkyoqy

Module 2: https://rebrand.ly/qy6nskd

Module 3: https://rebrand.ly/zttcyaa

Module 4: https://rebrand.ly/uc61haf

Module 5: https://rebrand.ly/a0832f0

Module 6: https://rebrand.ly/vjxt4c5

Module 7: https://rebrand.ly/zqkim8s

If you have trouble accessing any of the above video links, please contact us at Bill@Gospel-App.com

For more information or to dig deeper, check out www.takeheartyz.

"I have told you these things, so that in me you may have peace. In this world you will have trouble. But take heart! I have overcome the world."
(John 16:33 NIV)

"Whatever our failings may be, we need not lower our eyes in the presence of Jesus."
(Brennan Manning, The Ragamuffin Gospel)

Module #0: The Gospel App Shape

"And I pray that you, being rooted and established in love, may have power, together with all the saints, to grasp how wide and long and high and deep is the love of Christ, and to know this love that surpasses knowledge — that you may be filled to the measure of all the fullness of God. Now to him who is able to do immeasurably more than all we ask or imagine, according to his power that is at work within us…" (Eph 3:18-20 NIV)

The Gospel App Shape

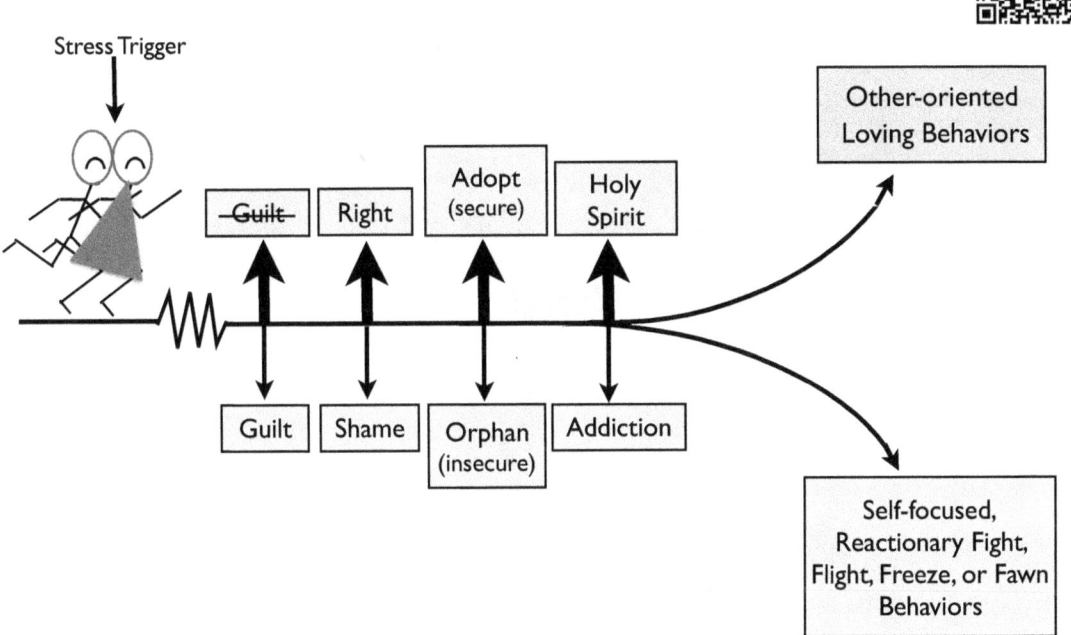

Notes:

Take heart

x

1 Module #1: Miraculous Faith

> "[This book] is for smart people who know they are stupid
> and honest disciples who admit they are scalawags."
> Brennan Manning, "The Ragamuffin Gospel"

The Simple Uncluttered Gospel

Jesus-Follower, strictly because of what Jesus did for you 2000 years ago, God must love you. He loves you as much as the Father loves the Son and the Son loves the Father—as you are, not as you should be or could be. You can't add to it, or take away from it. You cannot mess it up. I get it. Sometimes, maybe often, it doesn't feel like God loves you or you worry if you have disappointed Him. The Gospel says that He loves you right now as you are. How do you experience this love more? You can take simple Biblical baby-steps. Simply, ask the Holy Spirit in you to MAKE you experience the love of God for you right now.

Notes:

Honestly, the Gospel is _____ to believe on our own!

The Gospel is _____ than our imagination.

> "And I pray that you, being rooted and established in love,
> may have power, together with all the saints, to grasp how wide
> and long and high and deep is the love of Christ, and to know
> this love that surpasses knowledge
> — that you may be filled to the measure of all the fullness of God.
> Now to him who is able to do immeasurably more than all we ask or imagine,
> according to his power that is at work within us..."
> (Eph 3:18-20 NIV)

Take heart

What do I Need to Do in order to get God to really like me?

Circle the "good thing" below that if you did it more often or better, would cause your spiritual life to just take off.

- Pray more
- More silent retreats
- Gave more
- Attended church more
- Gave more to the poor
- Repented more
- Read Bible more
- Other "good" things

Truth? Because of what Jesus has done 2000 years ago, God can't like you any more than He does right now, even if you did more of the above.

The Simple Uncluttered Gospel App Shape (Part 1)

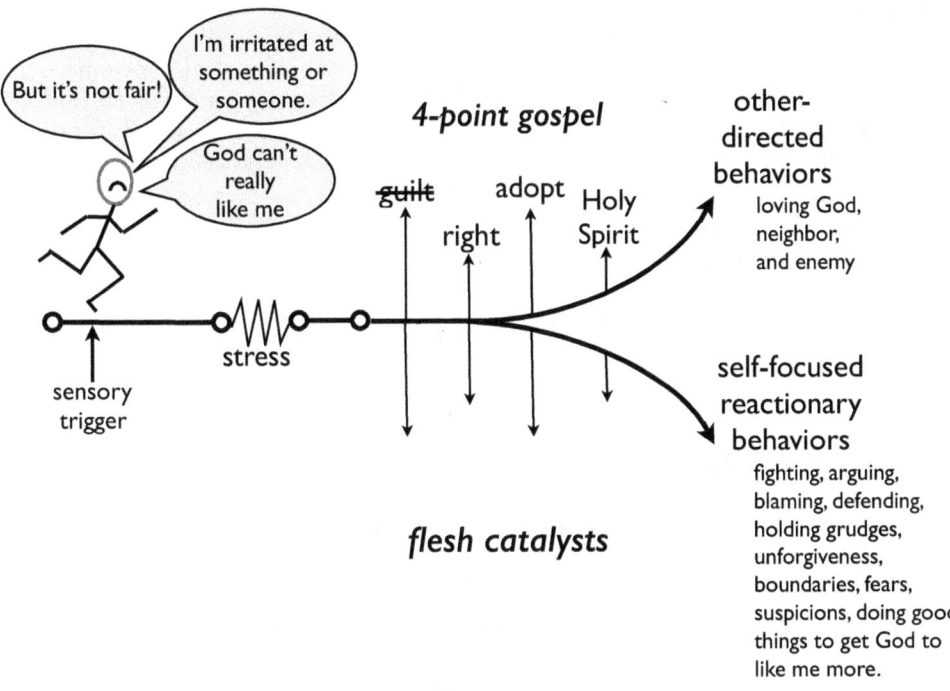

~~Guilt~~ (upward arrow #1)

Jesus Follower, 2000 years ago, Jesus did something remarkable for you. You had a trial. All of the things you did that were disappointing to God were put on trial. You were found guilty of celestial treason. The penalty was death.

Good news. Jesus took ALL of the punishment due you on the cross. It is finished.

Now God can never judge you again for anything. He cannot be critical or even disappointed in you. You can never be put on probation. He did all of that to Jesus on your behalf.

The Simple Uncluttered Gospel App Shape (cont.)

Right (upward arrow #2)

Jesus Follower, 2000 years ago, Jesus did something else remarkable for you. Jesus' life record of being absolutely faithful to God was mysteriously shoved into your official biographical record. Technically, you receive all that perfect faithfulness earns, including all of the love that the Father feels for the Son and the Son feels for the Father. He has to love you. He has to like you. He does, as you are right now, not as you could be or should be. Praise God!

You cannot add to it by doing more, or take away from it by doing less.

Adoption (upward arrow #3)

There's more. Jesus Follower, 2000 years ago, Jesus did something else remarkable for you.

You've been shoved into an unwavering, infinitely-secure relationship of honor as a full card carrying child of God in good standing. God is now your proud Father. Today He looks at you and says, "This is my beloved son/daughter, with whom I am well pleased"--all because of the work of Jesus on your behalf.

You cannot mess it up.

Holy Spirit (upward arrow #4)

(more to come next module!)

Just accept the Unimaginable!

What do you have to do to receive more of this? Nothing. You can't get any more than you have right now. Jesus earned it all and has passed it on to you. Now having said that, you can experience it more often. We will show you how.

"Rules of Engage-"

en·gage groups

What do Engagement groups look like?

First, what do Engagement groups not look like? They do not look like typical church or classroom settings where participants sit in rows facing forward listening to a single teacher—you know the old talking head approach—no judgment. The classroom format is most suitable for the mass transfer of information yet not effective for real engagement and dialogue between participants.

Instead, imagine participants gathered in circles of no more than 4-8 per circle. The groups gather around tables or simply chairs facing each other. We at Engage know that there is more to learning, particularly life-transforming learning, than just hearing someone else talk about it. We need to engage, to dialogue, to ask questions, to be able to disagree. Cool?

So we have prepared two or three Engage questions that should lead to great dialogue within the circles. They are generally designed to go deeper with each subsequent question. You get the idea. The first question is often "So share with the group something new that you learned about the Biblical text." Simple, no right or wrong answer, just, "Hey, what did you hear that you've never heard before?" Subsequent questions may ask for opinions, your thoughts, or even your feelings, You get it, right? We will be "taking the elevator down" a level. We want you to process what you heard and what the Spirit is telling you from within your own context and safe space. We are not looking for the "right answer."

How do we energize really safe and lively dialogue without the typical debating or that one Bible school graduate who always seems to know the right answer? That is the secret sauce of Engage.

So first, the facilitator lays out the question for discussion and hands off the first Engage question or statement to a particular person, by name, in each circle. "Betty, you get to go first. You have up to one minute to share your thoughts and feelings about this statement or question. Go."

While Betty is answering, the rest of the group is charged to intentionally listen. When Betty is done, she then passes the question to another person by name. "OK, Bob, you are next." Then Bob shares his thoughts, again, for no more than one minute and then passes the question off to another person who has not shared. This goes on until each person in the circle has had his or her opportunity to share what they are thinking.

By the way, anyone can opt out if they so choose, by saying "I would like to pass," and then passing the dialogue to the next participant by name. Cool?

After each one has been given the honor of sharing, the group goes to the second question, and so forth, until the end. There are usually two or three Engage questions in each lesson. In Engage-speak, as we said, the first question is usually very straight forward, subsequent questions are designed to "take the elevator down a level," that is to encourage deeper thought and more expression once people feel safe and have some skin in the game. For this to work, we must apply these Rules of Engagement. Please note,

This is not a place for debate.

This is not a place to divide into those who agree and those who disagree.

Please remain silent and attentive as others share.

This is not a place to show how smart or insightful you are.

This is not a place to ask clarification questions during or after a person shares. Feel free to go to coffee with that person at another time to chat more.

This is a good time to use "I" statements ("I believe," "I think," "I feel," "I see")

This is definitely a place to "take the elevator down a level" to be real and authentic. You may share fears, doubts, struggles, shame, addiction, your deep desires and wants and the like. Such vulnerability is key to relationship.

What is our goal in the Engage circles? This is a rare opportunity for real people who often have not found their place in such groups to have a safe place to deeply share, to intentionally listen and to honor the others in the group. It works.

Keep in mind that we don't want the group to be over burdened by strict heavy-handed rules and regulations. Not at all. Engage groups are meant to be free flowing and flexible and can be adapted to fit your particular context and denominational guidelines.

Engage Groups

Break up into your Engage groups. Remember, everyone will have up to one minute to share their thoughts. There is to be no criticism of others, or debate, or argumentation. Not here, please. The Engage questions are meant to be provocative and so there are definitely more than one way to answer them legitimately. Your answers are honored here.

Engage #1: What do you think? Is this too good to be true? Or are you comfortable with it? Have fun. Unpack your thoughts about this. Push back? Go for it.

Engage #2: Take a look at the partial Gospel App Shape on page 3. Talk about it. What makes sense? What needs clarification? What resonates with you in your context and relationships right now?

Engage #3: So read the simple uncluttered Gospel to yourself (on the first page of Module 1). What jumps off the page at you? Is something missing? Do you agree with it? Share your thoughts and feelings with the group. If it really were true, what difference might it make to your life right now? What would be noticeable to others?

Engage #4: So why doesn't God just fix me so that I can feel loved all the time? John Calvin wrestled with this as well.

"So why do believers feel such anxiety and fears related to their relationship with God? Why do we have so many violent temptations that just keep coming to our brains, unending wave after wave that inevitably cause us to doubt God's goodness, God's love for us, and our position as His child? Why doesn't faith give us more ongoing certainty? Why don't we just feel stunning confidence and assurance of God's adoration all the time? For reasons known only to God, this side of heaven, we are not promised a certainty and assurance of our relational attachment to God that is never affected by fears, doubt, shame or anxiety. We are saved into a lifetime of struggle with our dysfunctional consciences that spew out fears and doubts. This is our charge, to learn to be aware of our struggle and to lean into faith to overcome our inner doubts and fears more regularly. This side of heaven, our consciences will never be still of fear and anxiety-free." (Institutes 3.2.17 paraphrased)

What do you think?

The Simple Uncluttered Gospel App Shape Part 2

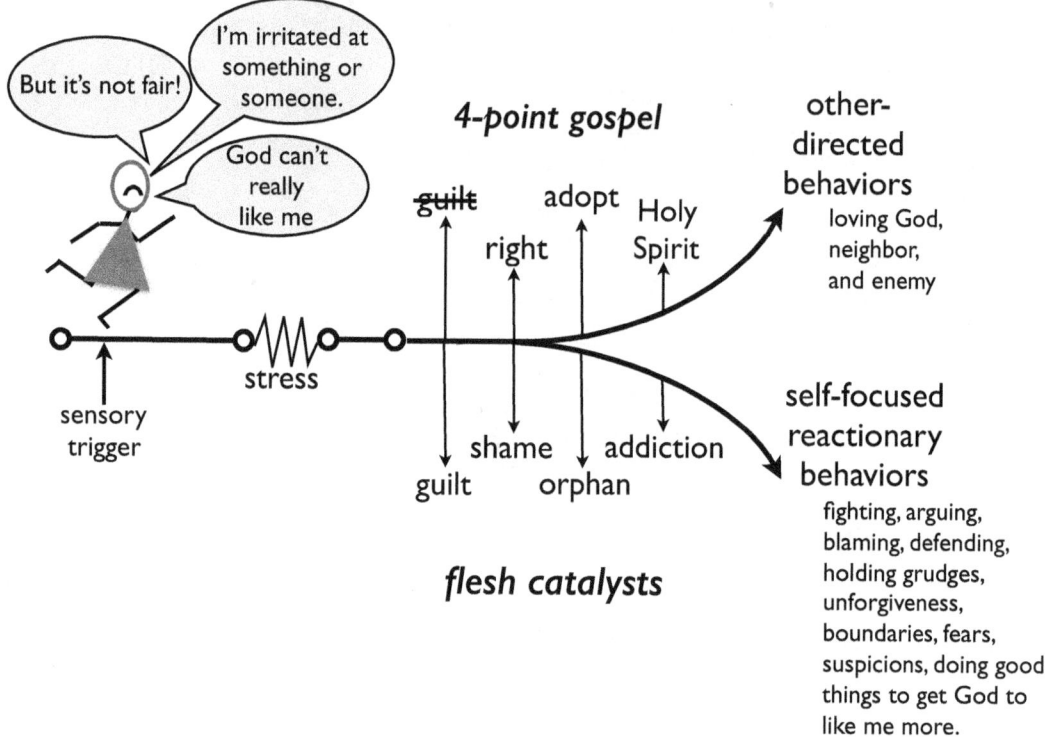

Notes:

Two Questions

1 What if you can't really believe? Not enough. What if everything that we said was true—you and I are so beat up, so insecure, so fearful, so paranoid, so riddled with hidden shame and guilt—and that's on a good day—that we can't really with great fervor embrace this truth, or hold onto it for any real length of time—not on our own power or capabilities anyway?

2 What if God knows this? God knows our wounds, scars, fears, and doubts? And has made a way, a provision, a path? And we have been largely ignorant of it. It is low hanging fruit. A little effort will make a noticeable difference.

Notes:

Preaching the Gospel to Myself

" God, I am feeling a little bit hopeful about this, more than I have been about anything religious recently. This is giving me new hope that I can feel Your love now. I confess that Jesus purchased that love for me. I have tried working harder—doing more good things—studying to learn what the Bible says—trying harder to believe more but received very little fruit from that related to You and me, me and You. Other times, I just gave up—quit. What was the point, I thought? OK, I am here, I am in the posture of receiving from you, not doing anything to earn, to manipulate, to cajole—my hands are open and upward. Holy Spirit give me your power to know how much You love me as I am, not as I should be. Holy Spirit, now please, give me Your faith, to really, really know that I am in the heavenly number, a person in good standing, no probation, no unfinished tasks ahead of me, loved by You with all of the love in the universe, in spite of my lack of experience of that lately, from You or others. I wait. Quickly please. I struggle so much now. "

Summary of Take Heart Sequel Module 1

1 The Gospel is so big, so other, so beyond our paygrade, so mysterious and inexplicable that it is naturally wildly wonderful and wildly troubling at the same time.

2 If you think that you have the Gospel down, or think that you have grasped its edges even with your arms wide open, you are greatly mistaken. It is so much bigger than you think. That is such good news.

3 Two questions remain:

1) What if you can't believe it today?

2) What if God knows that and has already made a path for you?

Miscellaneous Exercise: How Does the Gospel Hit Me Now?

Circle the image below that best represents how you respond to the mysteriousness and vast otherness of the Gospel. Have fun. Share your answer with someone.

Take heart

Want more?: Wrestling with the Gospel

Below are some likely and normal responses when people are confronted with the height, width, length, and depth of the Gospel and are invited to share their thoughts in a safe place. These are not evil explorations, only explorations. Consider each statement below and determine if you very much disagree, disagree, feel neutral, agree or very much agree. No right or wrong answers. Anything leap out at you? (5 minutes)

	Very Much Disagree		Neutral		Very Much Agree
I am comfortable with my understanding of my faith as is.	1	2	3	4	5
I find some of this frightening.	1	2	3	4	5
Why haven't I heard this before?	1	2	3	4	5
If this is true, I would have done things differently.	1	2	3	4	5
It is not clear what my part is in this relationship with Christ.	1	2	3	4	5
I have heard this before.	1	2	3	4	5
I find this confusing.	1	2	3	4	5
This kind of love does trouble me.	1	2	3	4	5
This stirs up a 1000 other questions.	1	2	3	4	5
This changes how I tell people about God's love.	1	2	3	4	5
I still think that I have messed up my relationship with God somewhat.	1	2	3	4	5
So, I can now do anything I want?	1	2	3	4	5

Thoughts?:

take heart

"It is by the Spirit alone that he daily unites himself to us. By the same grace and energy of the Spirit, we become His members, so that he keeps us under him, and we in our turn possess him."

"Therefore, as we cannot possibly come to Christ unless drawn by the Spirit, so when we are drawn we are both in mind and spirit exalted far above our own understanding. For the soul, when illumined by him, receives as it were a new eye, enabling it to contemplate heavenly mysteries, by the splendor of which it was previously dazzled. And thus, indeed, it is only when the human intellect is irradiated by the light of the Holy Spirit that it begins to have a taste of those things which pertain to the kingdom of God; previously it was too stupid and senseless to have any relish for them."

"Hence, in order that the word of God may gain full credit, the mind must be enlightened, and the heart confirmed, from some other quarter. We shall now have a full definition of faith, if we say that it is a firm and sure knowledge of the divine favor toward us, founded on the truth of a free promise in Christ, and daily revealed to our minds, and sealed on our hearts, by the Holy Spirit."

John Calvin on Faith and the Spirit
(Institutes 3, expanded and paraphrased)

Module #2: The Simple Uncluttered Gospel

"It is now proper to consider the nature of this faith, by means of which, those who are adopted into the family of God obtain possession of the heavenly kingdom. For the accomplishment of so great an end, it is obvious that no mere opinion or persuasion is adequate."
(John Calvin)

"For we are allured to seek God when told that our safety is treasured up in him; and we are confirmed in this when he declares that he studies and takes an interest in our welfare. Hence there is need of the gracious promise, in which he testifies that he is a propitious Father; since there is no other way in which we can approach him, the promise being the only thing on which the heart of man can recline."
(John Calvin)

The Simple Uncluttered Gospel

Pair off and say the Simple Uncluttered Gospel below aloud to someone else. Then sit back as they share it with you. This is a very good start to beginning to experience it more every day.

So What is the Simple Uncluttered Gospel?

"Jesus-Follower, strictly because of what Jesus did for you 2000 years ago, God has to love you. He does love you with all of His heart, as much as the Father loves the Son and the Son loves the Father. He can't love you any more or any less than He does right now. He loves you as you are, not as you should be or could be. You can't add to this love or take away from it.

Now, I get it, it often feels like you've messed it up or need to do something so that God would like you better. Not so! Good news, there is something that you can do, and are invited to do. You can take daily baby-steps to ask the Spirit inside of you to make you know, experience, and feel, just how much God loves you right now. Just ask. Ask later today. Ask tomorrow. Make it a spiritual habit."

(Eph 3:14-21, Rom 5:6-8, 1 Cor 13:4-8, John 13:34-35, Titus 2:11-13)

Take heart

Two Questions From Module 1

1 What if you can't really believe? Not enough. What if everything that we said was true—you and I are so beat up, so insecure, so fearful, so paranoid, so shame and guilt ridden—and that's on a good day— that we can't really, with great fervor, embrace this truth, or hold onto it for any real length of time—not on our own power or capabilities anyway?

2 What if God knows this? And He does. God knows our wounds, scars, fears, and doubts? And has made a way, a provision, a path? And we have been largely ignorant of it. Yet, it is low hanging fruit. A little effort will make a noticeable difference.

"So why do believers feel such anxiety and fears related to their relationship with God? Why do we have so many violent temptations that just keep coming to our brains, unending wave after wave that inevitably cause us to doubt God's goodness, God's love for us, and our position as His child? Why doesn't faith give us more ongoing certainty? Why don't we just feel stunning confidence and assurance of God's adoration all the time? For reasons known only to God, this side of heaven, we are not promised a certainty and assurance of our relational attachment to God that is never affected by fears, doubt, shame or anxiety. We are saved into a lifetime of struggle with our dysfunctional consciences that spew out fears and doubts. This is our charge, to learn to be aware of our struggle and to lean into faith to overcome our inner doubts and fears more regularly. This side of heaven, our consciences will never be still or fear and anxiety-free."
(John Calvin, Institutes 3.2.17 paraphrased and expanded)

Yeah, But What Do I *Do*?

Check out the following verses and identify the two answers to the question: How can I know God's crazy love for me as I am—not as I should be or could be—now? The highlighted prepositions (Greek: "dia" and "ek") should be read "by means of" or "through" —referring to instrumentality (here is where I get this, this is what makes _____ happen to me). So how can I really, really feel right now that God loves, and likes, me as I am? Two answers, and neither one is you trying harder or trying to work your believing-muscles more.

> I pray that out of his glorious riches [God] may strengthen you with power **through** [read: by means of] his Spirit in your inner being, so that Christ may dwell in your hearts **through** [read: by means of] faith. And I pray that you, being rooted and established in love may have power, together with all the saints, to grasp how wide and long and high and deep is the love of Christ, and to know this love that surpasses knowledge — that you may be filled to the measure of all the fullness of God.
> (Eph 3:16-19 NIV)

> And hope does not disappoint us, because God has poured out his love into our hearts **by** [read: by means of] the Holy Spirit, whom he has given us.
> (Rom 5:5 NIV)

> Those who obey his commands live in him, and he in them. And this is how we know that he lives in us: We know it **by** [read: by means of] the Spirit he gave us.
> (1John 3:24)

> We know that we live in him and he in us, because he has given us **of** [read: by means of] his Spirit.
> (1John 4:13)

What are the two lone means by which God has made it so that I will actually feel loved and liked by Him today, as I am, not as I should be?

1) The H_____ S_____ in me

2) F_____

Notice that such good things as "trying harder", "believing more", "doing more religious things" are NOT among the answers given by either Paul or John.

> "True spirituality is not a superhuman religiosity; it is simply true humanity released from bondage to sin and renewed by the Holy Spirit. This is given to us as we grasp by faith the full content of Christ's redemptive work: freedom from the guilt and power of sin, and newness of life through the indwelling and outpouring of his Spirit."
> (Richard Lovelace, Dynamics of Spiritual Life)

Take heart

Two Historic Approaches of Working With the Spirit

1 I just need to _____ more. ➡ Then God unleashes His blessings toward me again.

2 I ask the Spirit to give me His _____ ➡ It is His Faith alone that can make me feel God's love for me as I am right now (Gal 5:6). It also produces love in me for God and others.

Thoughts?:

"What is this faith in a nutshell? Faith is a firm and sure knowledge (beyond logic or our ability to reason) of the divine favor toward us, that is, how much He likes us, adores us, is proud of us, founded on the truth of a free promise in Christ, and revealed to our minds, and sealed on our hearts, by the Holy Spirit."

John Calvin, Institutes 3.2.7 (paraphrased and expanded)

"But the fruit of the Spirit is love, joy, peace, patience, kindness, goodness, [faith], gentleness and self-control. Against such things there is no law.
(Paul, Galatians 5:22-23)

The Holy Spirit's Secret Workings

The Holy Spirit is like a fountain whose passion is to make me believe right now, as I am, not as I should be, with no strings, that the first three upward aspects of the Gospel are true

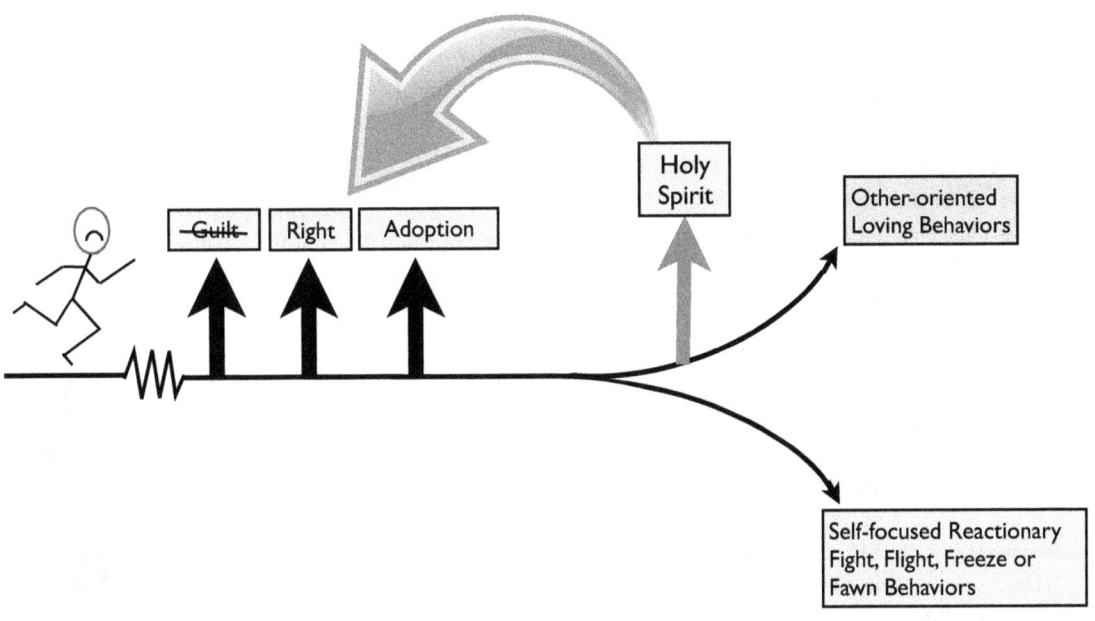

What can I do?
Ask the Holy Spirit in me to make me know, experience, get, feel, just how much God loves me, right now! Not perfectly. That's Heaven. But it should be noticeable.

"It is by the Spirit alone that he daily unites himself to us. By the same grace and energy of the Spirit, we become His members, so that he keeps us under him, and we in our turn possess him."
John Calvin, Institutes 3.1.3 (paraphrased and expanded)

"Therefore, as we cannot possibly come to Christ unless drawn by the Spirit, so when we are drawn we are both in mind and spirit exalted far above our own understanding. For the soul, when illumined by him, receives as it were a new eye, enabling it to contemplate heavenly mysteries, by the splendor of which it was previously dazzled. And thus, indeed, it is only when the human intellect is irradiated by the light of the Holy Spirit that it begins to have a taste of those things which pertain to the kingdom of God; previously it was too stupid and senseless to have any relish for them."
John Calvin, Institutes 3.3.34 (paraphrased and expanded)

take heart

Going Beyond with John Calvin

The following are paraphrased and expanded excerpts from John Calvin's Institutes of the Christian Religion on the relationship between "faith" and the Holy Spirit. It is very powerful must-read for all Jesus-Followers.

The Benefits of Christ Made Available to Us By The Secret Operation of the Spirit

This is very important. What is the main reason that God lavishes us with the same blessings He lavished His own Son? Not for our sakes as consumers, for our private use. Certainly not. No, it is so that we would be free and motivated to bless others, those who lack, those who need. Understand that we cannot get one microscopic bit of the blessings until we are mysteriously united with Jesus. He must become ours, in fact, He must dwell within us. So when we say that we access all of this by faith, we do not mean some casual mental agreement, by no means.

> We must see that it is only by the ongoing secret workings of the Spirit that we can ever enjoy the blessings of Christ. If not for the Spirit, we would never know the benefits of our salvation.

The Holy Spirit is the present glue by which Christ effectually binds us to Himself each and every day. (3.1.1)

Did you know this? The Holy Spirit in each of us is constantly busy subduing and destroying our many and varied lusts, our got-to-have-nows, while at the same time inflaming our hearts with the love of God and the motivation to want to do loving things toward God. Hence He receives the name of "Fire." He is also described to us as a "Fountain," as the source from which all heavenly riches flow to us; or as the "Hand" by which God exerts His power. By His divine inspiration He regularly breathes divine life into us so that we are no longer solely acted upon by our selfish desires, our dysfunctional and easily-deceived will, our habits and reactionary behaviors. Truth be told, our choices are heavily influenced by many things, some which clearly bypass our frontal cortices and its ability to reason and objectively choose. Each of us is riddled with blindspots, often relationally destructive reactionary behaviors, entrenched habits, not to mention fear and addiction cycles.

Yet, there is a new sheriff in town, within Jesus-Followers, that is. How do we know? His presence is evidenced by the new and different motivation and power we begin to see within us. It should be noticeable by others. Everything good in us is the fruit of His grace. Apart from His signature power and motivation, we are stuck with entrenched, often-dark neural pathways, and perverse destructive habits and behaviors. Until our brains are intentionally dependent upon the Spirit, Christ is, in a manner, unemployed. We look at Him a bit on the cold side, as if He were an outsider.

It is only by means of the Spirit's daily secret working in us, His grace and power—not by anything that we do—that He begins to make us feel united and somehow in-sync with Him. The Spirit alone makes us daily embrace Jesus. (3.1.3)

Is this mere theoretical hub-bub? Good question. Remember Adam and Cain and the trouble they each got into? They each had a choice. After the mess that their free wills caused, they could look up into God's eyes to find mercy and acceptance. But they didn't. They were too afraid of seeing just how angry and indignant God was toward them. They just knew that if they ever looked up, they would see it clearly in His gaze. That was a non-starter for them. Their shamed consciences would have just expected that God wasn't good with them—at all. Something inside them wouldn't look up, couldn't. So much for free wills.

So they could have really used this "faith" that comes from the Spirit. This Holy-Spirit-faith is far more powerful than the worst of guilt, shame and fear in our consciences. Spirit-faith reacts in just the opposite way. It makes the person want to look up into God's eyes, into His measuring gaze. Holy Spirit faith would have motivated them to not hide from His eyes. Well that would have been a whole other story. Wouldn't it?

What is this Holy-Spirit-faith in a nutshell?

> Faith that exclusively comes from the Spirit is a firm and sure knowledge (beyond logic or our ability to reason) of the divine favor toward us. It makes us know how much God likes us, adores us, is proud of us—as we are, right now, not as we should be. Such a mysterious and powerful Spirit-faith is not willy-nilly. No, it is founded on the truth of a free promise in Christ, and intentionally revealed to our minds, and sealed on our hearts by the Holy Spirit. (3.2.7)

This is the passion of the Spirit inside of Jesus-Followers. This should be observable to us and others.

So are there other "faiths?" Yes of course. There appear to be a variety of manifestations of faith by the Spirit, some less powerful and transformative than others. The pinnacle of the Spirit's manifestation can be experienced when I am actually enabled to cry, "Abba Father," as I am, not as I should be, whether it has been a good or a bad day for me. Others seem to receive a different faith, lets call it a faith-awareness of sorts but in truth what they have is more of a fading faith, a faith riddled in doubt and fears. I will call it "mini-faith." Though it has some similarities with Spirit-faith, it lacks any real power to change our motivations. Unlike the Spirit-faith, it will not perfect itself in time. Be warned. Such an inferior mini-faith remains a temptation even for actual believers. It can be quite addictive. Why? Because unlike Spirit-faith, we can do it on our own and quickly get dopamine hits from our brains.

> So, we must diligently teach Jesus-followers to regularly and carefully examine themselves, for it is very easy to fall back upon an inferior assurance, that mini-faith, which makes sense to their brains, but is powerless to rid anyone of daily doubts.

Here's a good way of putting it. As I said, beware of a faith that is too reasonable. If your faith makes sense to you, it is most likely the shadow counterfeit mini-faith. True faith is of the Spirit and so it is beyond reasonability (Eph 3:14-21). That is to say, it is beyond human explanation. It does not come from your head. Rather it is produced by the Spirit alone. Since it is above your paygrade, the only way to get it is to ask God for it every day. Mini-faith gives you no real assurance of your relationship with God. It has no power to diminish your innate doubts, fears, confusion, or anxieties. (3.2.11)

As I said, this heavenly faith is not a function of your brain's ability to know or comprehend. This Spirit-sourced faith is so vast and so far beyond your human ability to figure out that is it misleading to suggest that your brain could ever grab hold of it, even on your best day. In some ways it is right to say that Spirit-faith will always be confounding to your natural reason. Even when Spirit-faith engages you, your brain will still be woefully incapable of trying to explain it. And yet because of the nature of this Spirit-birthed-faith, at least for a few moments, you will be quite sure how much God loves you right now. You might even look up.

Hence, it is elegantly described by Paul as the power "together with all the saints, to grasp how wide and long and high and deep is the love of Christ, and to know this love that sur-passes knowledge (Eph 3:18, 19). Paul's object was to suggest that what our mind embraces by faith is in every way infinite and far beyond our frontal cortices finite capacity. The knowledge of this Spirit-faith far surpasses all ability of any brain to understand. And yet, now because of the Spirit, the "mystery which has been hid from ages and from generations" is now "made manifest to the saints," (Col 1: 26). A miracle takes place beyond our cognitive capacity and even over our reason's objections, and our doubts, fears, guilt, and shame.

It is unfortunate that we are limited to the same words to describe both "faiths." Due to the lack of better words, this faith-from-the-Spirit is occasionally termed in Scripture "understanding," (Col 2:2) and "knowledge," as by John, (1 John 3:2) when he declares that believers know themselves to be the sons of God. And certainly they do know, but this "knowing" is the result of an incomprehensible miracle of God, rather than something that your brain has figured out on its own or learned by some argument or Power Point presentation. Hence we conclude that this "knowledge" of Spirit-faith is more a result of imputed certainty rather than by inductive or deductive discernment. (3.2.14)

Faith Misappropriated

There are some who have things very confused. They know that God's mercy is great, and is showered upon many corporately, like the church, but are just not comfortable with God showering His mercy upon them individually. Experientially, on a day-to-day basis they imagine it out of their reach. So, "Spirit-faith may be for other people, but not for me." Maybe they are afraid that they have messed up too much, irreparably disappointed God so long ago, or feel that they deserve only punishment or discipline. Just beneath the surface, these men and women are sadly riddled and harassed by miserable fears, shame, doubts, and anxieties.

Yet this Spirit-faith that we speak of is good news to these really beat-up people and can come to their rescue, beyond their hopes and dreams. When they ask the Spirit to give them power to access this Spirit-faith, they receive a deep sense of "pleroforia," (Greek for "assurance") of how God feels toward them right now. How good is that? This heavenly pleroforia causes them to know, not only that God is good, or even that God is good to them. They will come to know that God loves them as they are, not as they should be. Their doubts, fears, and even shame are for a moment diminished some, not perfectly, that's heaven. But it is noticeable. This is beyond emotionalism. This is identity level awareness. This is the nature of Spirit-Faith alone. The same cannot be said of mini-faith at all.

Hence from this Spirit-faith, the Apostle deduces confidence, and from confidence boldness. His words are, "In [Christ] and through faith in Him we may approach God with freedom and confidence" (Eph 3:12). Makes sense, right?

Paul is arguing that my typical faith is of my own doing and choice unless one thing is evident. Does my "faith" enable me to calmly look up into God's measuring gaze expecting to be adored and honored as if I had been perfectly faithful? What an amazing miracle to know beyond my brain's ability to comprehend that this relationship is mine, eternally mine—that I cannot, nor have I, messed it up. Such miraculous, mysterious boldness springs only from this unreasonable pleroforia of God's favor toward me ignited by this heavenly Spirit-faith. So true is this, that the term "faith" is often used as equivalent to "confidence." (3.2.15)

So why do believers feel such anxiety and fears related to their relationship with God? Why do we have so many violent temptations that just keep coming to our brains, unending wave after wave that inevitably cause us to doubt God's goodness, God's love for us, and our position as His adored child? Why doesn't faith give us more certainty? Why don't we just feel stunning confidence and assurance of God's adoration all the time?

> For reasons known only to God, this side of heaven, we are not promised a certainty and assurance of our relational attachment to God that is never affected by fears, doubt, shame, or anxiety. We are saved into a lifetime of struggle with our dysfunctional consciences that spew out fears and doubts.

This is our charge, to learn to be aware of our struggle and to lean into Spirit-sourced faith to overcome our inner doubts and fears more regularly. This side of heaven, our consciences will never be still, or fear and anxiety-free. (3.2.17)

Two Paths

There are two paths for the believer, the path of the Spirit and the path of the Flesh.

On the Spirit's path the believer is filled with delight in God's goodness toward him or her. On the Flesh's path, the believer is filled with bitterness.

On the Spirit's path, the Christian finds surprising comfort and security in the promises in the Gospel. Not so on the Flesh's path. On those hard cobblestones there is only guilt, shame and fear—wondering if God has turned away.

On the Spirit's path is the profound anticipation of life; on the lesser path, fear of death.

These paths are available no matter what is happening in the believer's life, whether their lot is hard or easy here.

Why the two paths? Why doesn't God just fix it so that we can only take the higher path?

> For reasons unknown, we are relegated to struggle with hearts that are redeemed yet still diseased with distrust. We are innately unable or unwilling to fully embrace the heavenly life-changing faith that is distrust's only supernatural predator.

In our brains, this side of heaven, certainty is always mingled with doubt. There is no perfect respite here. The perfect Spirit-faith that has penetrated our being, due to the ongoing daily efforts of the Holy Spirit in us, is only a tiny fraction of the faith that will eventually be ours. So for now, though perfect, Spirit-faith alone will not let us perfectly apprehend just how much God adores us as we are. It is a perfect faith, but our access of it is intentionally incomplete. Our experience of God's feeling toward us—this side of Heaven—will always be obscured and confused to some degree.

The good news is that no matter how bad it gets in our journey, no matter how much oppression, dehumanization, loneliness, mistreatment, no matter how agitated and distrustful we may become in the moment, the substance of that Spirit-faith remains. Once engaged, always engaged. That heavenly faith, in contrast to other "mini-faiths," will eventually overcome all of the difficulties. Be assured of that. (3.2.18)

This unique Spirit-faith that we speak of, birthed of God alone, is very powerful. The very moment that the most miniscule shard of faith engages our brains, we begin to really see the smiling face of God toward us. In His measuring eyes we now see His peacefulness, gentleness, and favor toward us. It is not a dream at all. Somehow Spirit-faith makes us aware that it is the real deal and that it is ours.

Yet to be clear, we cannot grasp it all. This side of heaven we are surrounded by a cloud of ignorance and obscurity related to this Spirit-faith and the vastness of God's favor toward us. Yet we are also made aware that the little assurance of God's love for us that we do feel is very real and will without a doubt grow in the days to come.

Here's a good word picture. Imagine a prisoner who can see the sun's rays through a narrow crack in his cell. He is deprived of a full view of the sun, and cannot benefit from experiencing it in freedom without hindrance. Yet he still has no doubt that it is the sun's light. He has no doubt that there is more there once he is set free from his imprisonment. So too, though we know that there is far more to faith and the favor of God toward us, we just know-beyond-knowing that this is the real deal and we are secure in the hope that one day we will get it all. All of this is the result of the power of the Holy Spirit working daily in us. (3.2.19)

When Paul writes "For we know in part and we prophesy in part" (1 Cor 13:9), and

Take heart

"Now we see but a poor reflection as in a mirror" (1 Cor 13:12), he is communicating that whether we think so or not, we have been given only a miniscule particle of God's wisdom now, not the whole thing. To be clear, this is not to say that our Spirit-faith is faulty or corrupt. No, it is perfect, but given to us in a measured amount this side of heaven. It is far too big for us to swallow whole now. Paul concludes that this is our lot this side of Heaven. Each of us, so drastically under-equipped, is slower and far more challenged than we want to admit. We just never seem to get as close to God as we want.

Cheer up, Jesus-Follower, the small portion of Spirit-faith that you do have is sure, not corrupt, or broken, or deceptive. Paul again, "And we, who with unveiled faces all reflect the Lord's glory, are being transformed into His likeness with ever-increasing glory, which comes from the Lord, who is the Spirit" (2 Cor 3:18). Look, even a minute sliver of Spirit-faith accessed from the Spirit in us, should make an observable difference in our sense of significance, security and belonging. This cannot be said for mini-faith.

Now we see why we must struggle to depend upon Jesus 24/7, 365 days a year. We are encompassed 24/7, 365 days a year by such a natural stupor of ignorance, fears, and doubt. This is what our fallen-nature, even our redeemed fallen nature does. This downward spiral is exacerbated by our deeply entrenched guilt, shame, relational attachment issues, and addictions. Why is the struggle so hard? It is complicated, but certainly at the top of the list would be our heart which is innately biased and quite prone to unbelief. No one wants to admit that, but there it is. Also there are the infinite swarms of temptations that are often violent and oppressive.

If you are like me, your conscience, which remains so overwhelmed with conscious and subconscious guilt, will far too often groan and complain of its lot, or in shame accuse and hate itself, or even whisper conspiracies against God and others like a little terrorist cell inside our brain. Me too, no judgment.

Here is what happens all too often. When your dysfunctional conscience perceives that you are in a bad place, feeling beat up, abandoned, demeaned, treated unfairly, or unloved, or you think that God is for some reason disappointed in you and has turned away in disgust, it will almost automatically fall back to imagining that God is your enemy, not your beloved. Habitual reactionary emotions such as anxiousness and avoidance will ignite in your brain, and you will most likely act out like a sullen, self-focused two-year old. It is fear and unbelief to be sure. Instead of immediately looking up and begging for Spirit-faith, you will follow in the tragic footsteps of Cain and Adam before you. Like them, in fear and shame, you will look away from the eyes of God. Push comes to shove, unless there is regular intervention by some external power, your redeemed conscience will quickly tend to act out of fear toward God. This is your lot this side of heaven. Mine too.

What can you do to withstand these assaults? Simple. Ask to access Spirit-faith. This faith arms and fortifies itself with the word of God.

When the temptation comes—and it will—conspiring with your innate paranoia that God is your enemy because He either ordains or allows dehumanizing, unloving afflictions, and harm, do not fret. Then quickly ask the Holy Spirit to give you His faith. He will, you know. When it falls upon you, don't fight it. Spirit-faith will give you solace in a higher confounding truth, that while He afflicts—or allows affliction, suffering, or injustice, He is merciful. He can't love you any more than He does right now. I get it. It doesn't always feel like it. Yet His chastening of His children proceeds from love not anger. The natural mind, absent of such Spirit-faith can make no sense of this whatsoever. Mini-faith can only ultimately lead to bitterness, resentment, unbelief and anger. (3.2.20-21)

The Word is clear. Only this Spirit-sourced faith, which we speak of, by nature apprehends the love of God toward us. It has the innate capacity to place the promises of present and future life right in front of our eyes and to make us believe the ample security and comfort that is ours from the promised blessings (Eph 2:14).

Yet, this faith never promises you old age, health, success, or comfort here. The Lord has not promised these to you. Don't miss this. Spirit-faith in you is, by its nature, fully satisfied with God's assurances, that no matter how difficult your life is, God will never fail you. Once again, we are not making this stuff up out of hand. Faith's hope and assurance is firmly in God's promises, the Word.

So, Child of God, no matter how hard your life has been, what you've done or not done, or what's been done to you, the bad cards that you've been dealt in this world, God's favor toward you is not diminished at all. It may feel like it, but you are headed to complete and total happiness in the arms of your Heavenly Father who adores you as you are right now. Only this faith-that-exclusively-comes-from-the-Spirit can make you really know this is so, right now.

To be clear, how can you grasp this hope now? First, God says so in His word. Second, you can by this heavenly faith, right now be made very aware of God's remarkable favor toward you. Just ask. It is that favor that sources the blessings that are now yours and to a large extent being held for you in Heaven. (3.2.28)

Excerpts from
John Calvin's Institutes of The Christian Religion Book 3, Section 2,
(paraphrased and expanded by Dr. Bill Senyard)

Thoughts?:

Going Deeper: J. Gresham Machen on Faith

"When we come to see that what Paul calls the flesh is a mighty power, which is dragging us resistlessly down into an abyss of evil that has no bottom, then we feel our guilt and misery, then we look about for something stronger to help us than our own weak will. Such a power is found by Apostle Paul in faith; it is faith, he says, that produces or works itself out in, the life of love.

But what does Paul mean when he says that "faith works?" Certainly he does not mean what the modern pragmatist skeptic means when he uses the same words; certainly he does not mean that it is merely faith, considered as a psychological phenomenon, and independent of the truth or falsehood of its object, that does the work.

What he does mean is made abundantly clear in the last section of this same Epistle to the Galatians, where the life of love is presented in some detail. In that section nothing whatever is said about faith; it is not faith that is there represented as producing the life of love but the Spirit of God; the Spirit is there represented as doing exactly what, in the phrase "faith working through love," is ascribed to faith. The apparent contradiction leads us on to the right conception of faith. True faith, strictly speaking, does not do anything; it does not give, but receives. So when one says that we do something by faith that is just another way of saying that we do nothing—at least that we do nothing of ourselves.

It is of the very nature of faith, strictly speaking, to do nothing. So when it is said that faith works through love, that means that through faith, instead of doing something for ourselves we allow someone else to help us. That force which enters our life at the beginning through faith, before we could do anything at all to please God, and which then strengthens and supports us in battle that it has enabled us to begin, is the power of the Spirit of God.

The Christian preacher, then, comes before the world with a great alternative. Shall we continue to depend upon our own efforts, or shall we receive by faith the power of God? Shall we content ourselves with the materials which this world affords, seeking by endlessly new combinations to produce a building that shall endure; or shall we build with the materials that have no flaw? Shall we give men new motives, or ask God to give them a new power? Shall we improve the world, or pray to God to create a new world? The former alternatives have been tried and found wanting: the best of architects can produce no enduring building when all the materials are faulty; good motives are powerless when the heart is evil. Struggle as we may, we remain just a part of this evil world until, by faith, we cry: 'Not by might, nor by power, but by Thy Spirit, O Lord of Hosts.'"

(J. Gresham Machen, Faith and Works)

"The reception of that gift is faith: faith means not doing something, but receiving something; it means not the earning of a reward but the acceptance of a gift. A man can never be said to obtain a thing for himself if he obtains it by faith; indeed to say that he obtains it by faith is only another way of saying that he does not obtain it for himself but permits another to obtain it for him. Faith in other words, is not active but passive; and to say that we are saved by faith is to say that we do not save ourselves but are saved only by the one in whom our faith is reposed."

(J. Gresham Machen, Faith and Works)

Preaching the Gospel to Myself

> God, I am feeling a little bit more hopeful about this, more than I have been about anything religious recently. This is giving me new hope that I can feel Your love now. I confess that Jesus purchased that love for me. I have tried working harder—doing more good things—studying to learn what the Bible says—trying harder to believe more but received very little fruit from that related to You and me, me and You. Other times, I just gave up—quit. What was the point, I thought? OK, I am here, I am in the posture of receiving from you, not doing anything to earn, to manipulate, to cajole—my hands are open and upward. Holy Spirit give me your power to know how much You love me as I am, not as I should be. Holy Spirit, now please, give me Your faith, to really, really know that I am in the heavenly number, a person in good standing, no probation, no unfinished tasks ahead of me, loved by You with all of the love in the universe, in spite of my lack of experience of that lately from You or others here. I wait. Quickly please. I struggle so much now.

Summary of Take Heart Week 2

1 The passion and the secret working of the Holy Spirit in me is to make me believe that God loves me right now, as I am, not as I should be or could be, whether I am pursuing Him or not. The Holy Spirit is internally pursuing me all the time, 24/7, to make me feel like an adopted child.

2 Biblical faith, the capacity to really embrace that the Gospel is real and true for me right now, is a FRUIT of the Holy Spirit, not anything innate to me, or from me. I can ask for it. I can receive it. There are no mental or emotional muscle groups that make me "faith" more. This is very counter-cultural.

3 According to Paul in Galatians 5:6, it's the Holy Spirit's faith that makes love happen. The Holy Spirit's faith alone makes me feel the height, width, length, and depth of the love of Christ for me—and the height, width, length, and depth of the love of Christ for others through me.

take heart

"Here I must grab hold of the Simple Uncluttered Gospel, which teaches me, not what I ought to do, (for that is the wheelhouse of the Law), but what Jesus Christ the Son of God has already completed on my behalf. What is that? He suffered and died to deliver me from sin and death. The Simple Uncluttered Gospel desires that I would merely receive and believe that all of the prerequisites of the Law are done. This Simple Uncluttered Gospel is the principal article of all Christian doctrine. Do you want to know more about what godliness looks like? Simple, get to know the Simple Uncluttered Gospel well, teach it unto other Jesus-Followers, and beat it into their heads continually."

Martin Luther, Paul's Letter to the Galatians (paraphrased)

Module #3: Miraculous Relationships

> "By this all men will know that you are my disciples, if you love one another."
> (John 13:35)

> "Your mission Jim, should you choose/decide to accept it...As always, should you or any of your I.M.F. Force be caught or killed, the Secretary will disavow any knowledge of your actions. This tape/disc will self-destruct in five seconds. Good luck, Jim."
> Mission Impossible

> "By this, all men will know that you are my disciples, if you love one another."
> John 13:35

The Simple Uncluttered Gospel

"Jesus-Follower, strictly because of what Jesus did for you 2000 years ago, God loves you as much as the Father loves the Son and the Son loves the Father, as you are, not as you should be or could be. You can't add to this love, or take away from it. You can't mess it up. Yet, I get that it doesn't always feel like it. Me too. No judgment."

"This [Simple Uncluttered Gospel] is the principal article of all Christian doctrine. Do you want to know more about what real godliness looks like? Simple, get to know the [Simple Uncluttered Gospel] well, teach it to other Jesus-Followers, and beat it into their heads continually."

Martin Luther- Letter to the Galatians (paraphrased)

Gospel App Shape

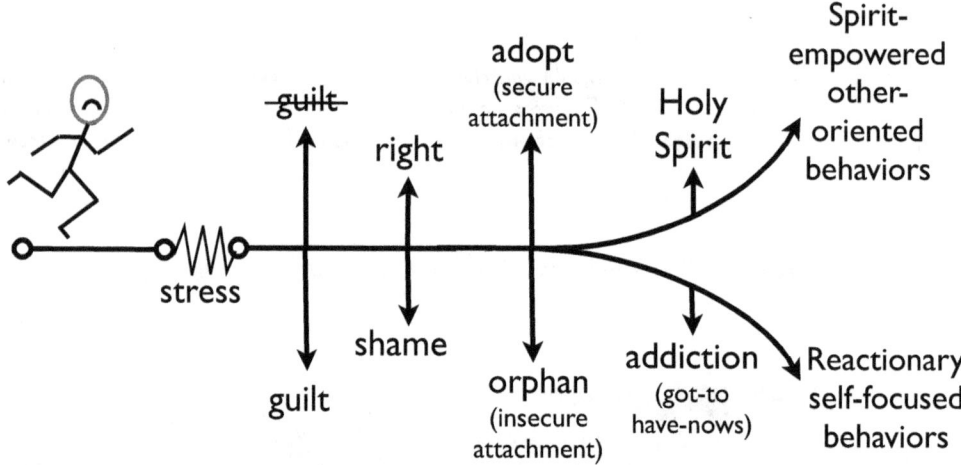

Pick one person, a Christian (at least you think so), with whom you are struggling relationally. Write his or her name, or initials, or code name in the blank below.

_____

Galatians 5:6 Spectrum

For in Christ Jesus neither circumcision nor uncircumcision has any value. The only thing that counts is faith expressing itself through love. (Gal 5:6 NIV)

"For in Christ Jesus whether you get circumcised or refuse the law and stay uncircumcised —neither choice has the capability to accomplish anything…" (5:6a paraphrased)

```
  1              3              5
not be                          be
circumcised                     circumcised
```

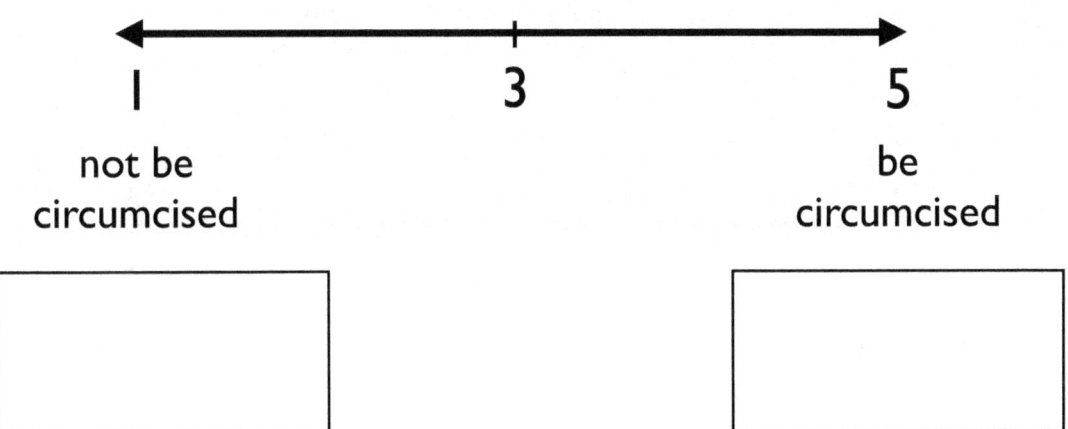

Credits to Serge.org for their brilliant exegesis and application of this verse in their Sonship curriculum. Check it out!

Galatians 5:6 Spectrum (cont.)

...The only thing that counts is faith expressing itself through love. (Gal 5:6 NIV)

"...On the other hand, the only thing that works is "faith" which actually makes love happen."
(paraphrase)

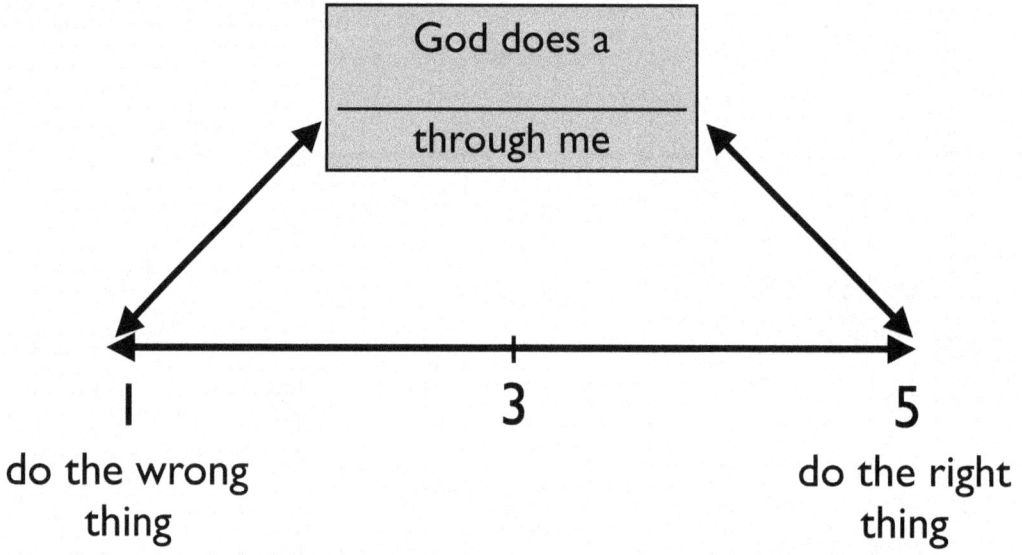

Loving Your Neighbor Spectrum (Galatians 5:6) cont.

"But I tell you who hear me: Love your enemies, do good to those who hate you."
(Luke 6:27)

"For in Christ Jesus whether you get circumcised or refuse the law and stay uncircumcised
—neither choice has the capability to accomplish anything.
On the other hand, the only thing that works is 'faith,'
which actually makes love happen."
Galatians 5:6 (alt translation)

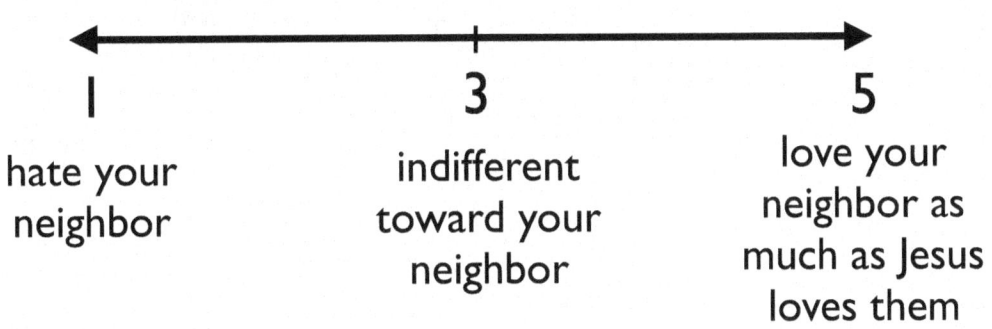

1	3	5
hate your neighbor	indifferent toward your neighbor	love your neighbor as much as Jesus loves them

For those of you who are actually in Christ, whether you choose to do the right thing and try to stretch your thin, thin Saran wrap thick love over the porcupiny other(s)—or whether you choose the opposite, just hate them, accuse them, justify your anger and rage, avoid them, slander them to others, or silently hope that they get crushed—in a real sense doesn't matter. Neither extreme has the capacity to accomplish loving the other, meaning, making you actually want to love them, or having them feel loved. The Kingdom is not furthered at all. Don't think that because you do a thing that looks like a loving thing (i.e., choose to forgive, choose to be compassionate, or choose to pursue) that you actually love the other person, or have the power to restore them, or forgive them, or reconcile with them, or to want to die for them, or that your love will change them in anyway. It won't. It does not have the power...

Gal 5:6 Paraphrase (Take Heart Sequel 3)

Loving Your Neighbor Spectrum (Galatians 5:6) cont.

Fortunately, there is another way for Spirit-filled Jesus followers like you. The Holy Spirit in you can overwhelm you with powerful superhuman faith—His fruit—His faith--that innately is all about one thing—making you feel the love that Jesus paid for and to feel a deep love for God and other people—including enemies. That is what the Holy Spirit's faith does. His faith makes love for others happen within you and has more than a decent shot at making it felt---at least noticed-- by the other.

So if you don't really love someone that God really loves, you have a legit choice. You can admit that such a love that loves regularly unloving and unlovable folk—a strange, dangerous and higher love, a miraculous love, a transforming love—is just not in your tool-box. Never was. However, as a Jesus-follower, you can ask the Holy Spirit to fill you with His Fruit of Faith, which will motivate and empower you to actually feel love for the other. They may actually feel that. They should feel a real difference. It's your choice. This is the love that Jesus spoke about that people will see and say, "Hey, he/she is a follower of Jesus. How else would they do that?" Please, stop thinking and bragging that, on your own, you are loving them with the love that God commands. Nothing could be further from the truth. Honestly, how's what you have been doing been working for you?

Gal 5:6 Paraphrase (Take Heart Sequel 3)

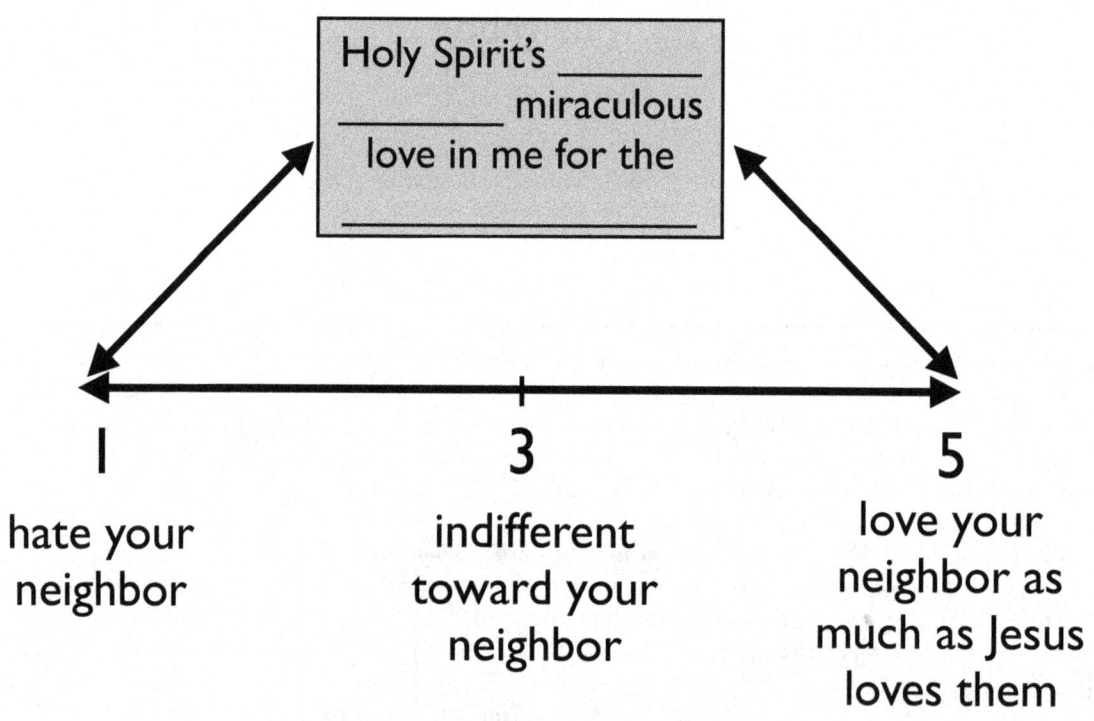

Engage Groups

Break up into your Engage groups. Remember, everyone will have up to one minute to share their thoughts. There is to be no criticism of others, or debate, or argumentation. Not here, please. The Engage questions are meant to be provocative and so there are definitely more than one way to answer them legitimately. Your answers are honored here.

Engage #1: Thinking of the person or situation that you brought to the table today, please share what you have tried to do to "love" them. How's it going for you and them? Again, no judgment here.

Engage #2: Apply Gal 5:6 to the current relational struggle that you brought up on page 30. Keep it confidential. This is not a place to air grievances. Fill in the blanks in the altered translation of Gal 5:6 in your workbook and read it aloud to the group. Use initials or abbreviations, or false name to protect the other party.

Whether I love _____, or despise, hate, avoid, feel anger toward, am still-faced, or indifferent toward them, nothing is going to really change. God is not any more pleased with me. There is no miraculous life-changing manifestation of the love of Christ either. No Gospel message. On the other hand, I can stop what I have been attempting to do in the name of right, or justification and plead with the Holy Spirit to give me His love for them, His love "through" me. That can actually change things. I now see that only His "faith" manufactured love can really change the relationship between me and _____.

What difference might you notice if such a miracle happened? What might they observe or feel? What are the "Yeah, buts…" that rush into your head? Isn't this a bit scary? Why?

take heart

What's Our Take-Away?

Here's What I Can Tell You About That Jesus-Follower Whom You Despise or Resent

Strictly because of what Jesus did for them 2000 years ago, God loves them as much as the Father loves the Son and the Son loves the Father. He can't love them any more or any less. He loves them now as much as He would if they hadn't hurt you. He loves them as much as He loves the Son even if they never repent or apologize to you or restore what they took from you.

Preaching the Gospel to Myself

> " God, right now I am hurting, depressed, angry, feeling disrespected, unloved, hopeless, beat-up, ashamed and feel like a failure…and that's just the tip of the iceberg. I really don't like this person. I wish I never knew them. To some degree, I despise them. I am also afraid of them. I can't take it being with them, being near them anymore. My body has a visceral reaction when I am in the same room. Honestly, I am at the end of my rope. I admit that You love them as they are, even after all the things they did to me, the many things they didn't do for me. I don't. I confess that I am way out of sync with You—in fact, this frightens me. Honestly, I am afraid that You can make me love them again. I am not sure at all that I want that to happen. I am done. However, I am willing to come to You to ask that You make me feel loved by You again. I need that. I want that desperately. Holy Spirit, unleash Your faith in my inner-being and make love happen for me. Now please. Amen. "

{addendum for when you are ready}

> " I am also begging that You give me Your love for them. This is hard right now. I am not so sure that I really want it. This is pretty scary. So give me Your perfect love that casts out fears. Give me wisdom so I don't go and do something stupid. Amen. "

Summary of Take Heart Week 3

1 Neither you nor I can love others…not like Jesus did or commands us to do. It would take a miracle.

2 The miracle has already been purchased for you, Jesus follower, and is available through the Holy Spirit in you by Faith.

3 How do I get such Faith? I ask. "You do not have, because you do not ask God. (James 4:2 NIV)

Take heart

Module #4: Miraculous Forgiveness For Others

> Alice: "A whippin', that's all they get after all they done?"
> Little Bill: "A whippin' ain't no little thing, Alice."
>
> — Unforgiveness (1992)

> Then Peter came to Jesus and asked, "Lord, how many times shall I forgive my brother when he sins against me? Up to seven times?" Jesus answered, "I tell you, not seven times, but seventy-seven times."
>
> — Matt 18:21-22 NIV

I Can't Forgive (Fill in the blanks)

I still can't forgive _____ for _____
_____

Take heart

But I Have Been Trying to Forgive!

Look, you are human. There are no forgiving muscle groups that you can rely on or exercise to get better at it. There are also subconscious powers centered in your flesh that are fighting against your desire to forgive. Consider the following statements below. Related to the situation that you are wrestling with right now, how do you feel about the statement? Do you very much disagree, feel indifferent, or very much agree. Be honest. No right or wrong answer. (5 minutes)

	Strongly Disagree		Neutral		Strongly Agree
1) I messed up too. It is partly my fault.	1	2	3	4	5
2) I forgive them, but I will not be nice to them as if it never happened.	1	2	3	4	5
3) Why do these things just happen to me?	1	2	3	4	5
4) I will pursue justice. I am due that.	1	2	3	4	5
5) I've done the same or similar thing to others.	1	2	3	4	5
6) Vengeance sounds pretty good to me.	1	2	3	4	5
7) God didn't stop it. He must feel the same way toward me?	1	2	3	4	5
8) They must show sorrow to my satisfacton for what they did.	1	2	3	4	5
9) I deserved it to some degree.	1	2	3	4	5
10) I have put up boundaries. They will not hurt me again.	1	2	3	4	5
11) I could have stopped the crime. I didn't.	1	2	3	4	5
12) What's wrong with me that I can't forgive?	1	2	3	4	5
13) I am supposed to forgive, but I have not.	1	2	3	4	5
14) Someone explain why this was fair! Nothing will move forward until we are even.	1	2	3	4	5
15) I will move on with my life.	1	2	3	4	5
16) I have found other ways to diminish my hurt feelings without them.	1	2	3	4	5

> Follow the instructions to calculate your possible forgiveness hindrances and graph them on the Gospel App shape on the next page.
> _____Guilt: Add your answers to statements 1, 5, 11 and 13.
> _____Shame: Add you answers to statements 3, 7, 9 and 12.
> _____Orphan Bent: Add your answers to statements 2, 4, 10 and 15.
> _____Addictions: Add your answers to statements 6, 8, 14 and 16.

Can't Forgive Graph

*P*ut your guilt, shame, insecure attachment and got-to-have-now forgiveness hindrance numbers on the appropriate vertical scales below with an "x." Then draw lines between each "x." Does this give you a helpful visual insight as to why it has been so hard to forgive the crime in question? Now, circle the item in the reactionary behavior list (far lower right) that best describes your go to strategy to date. Please share it with the group if you feel comfortable. (5 minutes)

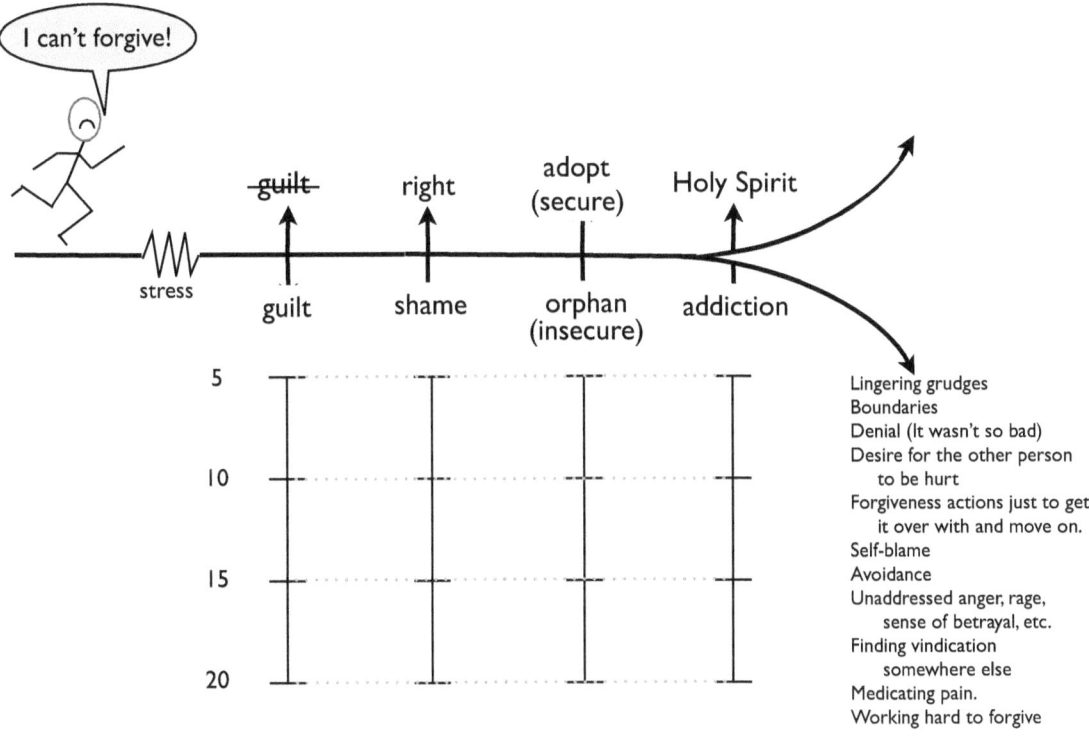

Lingering grudges
Boundaries
Denial (It wasn't so bad)
Desire for the other person to be hurt
Forgiveness actions just to get it over with and move on.
Self-blame
Avoidance
Unaddressed anger, rage, sense of betrayal, etc.
Finding vindication somewhere else
Medicating pain.
Working hard to forgive

Thoughts?:

Cupology 101

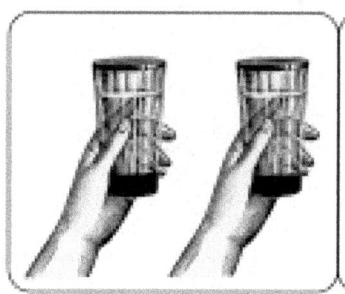  

Notes:

Bible Study: The Magnanimous King and the Boneheaded Servant

"21 Then Peter came to Jesus and asked, "Lord, how many times shall I forgive my brother or sister who sins against me? Up to seven times?" 22 Jesus answered, "I tell you, not seven times, but seventy-seven times.

23 "Therefore, the kingdom of heaven is like a king who wanted to settle accounts with his servants. 24 As he began the settlement, a man who owed him ten thousand bags of gold was brought to him. 25 Since he was not able to pay, the master ordered that he and his wife and his children and all that he had be sold to repay the debt. 26 "At this the servant fell on his knees before him. "Be patient with me," he begged, "and I will pay back everything." 27 The servant's master took pity on him, canceled the debt and let him go.

28 "But when that servant went out, he found one of his fellow servants who owed him a hundred silver coins. He grabbed him and began to choke him. "Pay back what you owe me!" he demanded. 29 "His fellow servant fell to his knees and begged him, "Be patient with me, and I will pay it back." 30 "But he refused. Instead, he went off and had the man thrown into prison until he could pay the debt.

31 When the other servants saw what had happened, they were outraged and went and told their master everything that had happened. 32 "Then the master called the servant in. "You wicked servant," he said, "I canceled all that debt of yours because you begged me to. 33 Shouldn't you have had mercy on your fellow servant just as I had on you?" 34 In anger his master handed him over to the jailers to be tortured, until he should pay back all he owed.

35 "This is how my heavenly Father will treat each of you unless you forgive your brother or sister from your heart." (Matt 18:21-35)

Notes:

Notes:

"forgive, cancel"
Greek aphieimi: to release from legal or moral obligation or consequence, cancel, remit, pardon debt--to forgive, give up any future justice or restitution.

"pity..."
Greek splagchnizomai: compassion, pity. Used only of God literally or metaphorically. It is God's innate, emotional, gut-wrenching motivation to redeem, love, honor, restore, set free people that He is committed to. It is God's "all-in."

"from your heart"
Jesus is making a distinction between an act of forgiveness and a motivation, or desire to forgive that comes from your heart. Peter had asked more generically--perhaps referring to a rational and intentional choice to forgive because it was the right thing to do. Jesus ups the stakes saying that what God demands is that we should want to set those who hurt us free. A very high bar.

Engage Groups

Break up into your Engage groups and process the parable. Remember, everyone will have up to one minute to share their thoughts. There is to be no criticism of others, or debate, or argumentation. Not here, please. The Engage questions are meant to be provocative and so there are definitely more than one way to answer them legitimately. Your answers are honored here.

Engage #1: In your experience, in real life, what might you have expected the King to say to the blockheaded totally irresponsible servant after the failed audit?

Engage #2: What got into the King so that he took a different path? What might some unintended consequences be from his outlandish approach to dealing with grossly incompetent, undependable, perhaps unethical and irresponsible servants?

Engage #3: What is the moral to Jesus' parable?

Splagchnizomai (pronounced: splangk-neetz-oh-my)

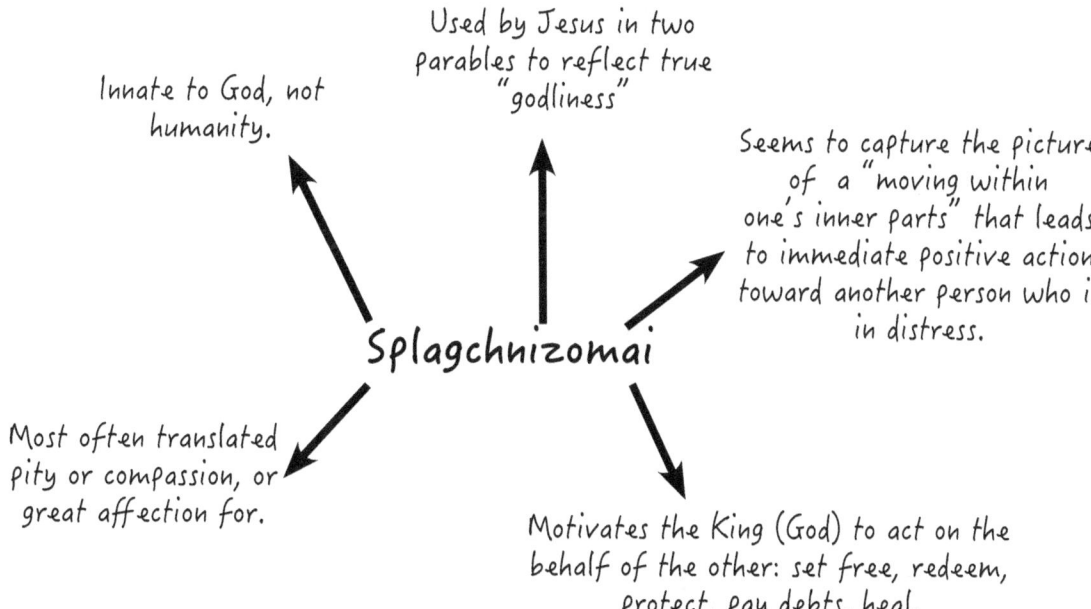

Biblical Splagchnizomai Verses:

"But a Samaritan, as he traveled, came where the man was; and when he saw him, he [splagchnizomai'd] him." (Luke 10:33)

"When Jesus landed and saw a large crowd, he felt [splagchnizomai toward] them and healed their sick." (Matt 14:14)

When the Lord saw her, he felt [splagchnizomai toward] her and he said, 'Don't cry.'" (Luke 7:13)

"I feel [splagchnizomai toward] these people; they have already been with me three days and have nothing to eat." (Mark 8:2)

"It has often thrown him into fire or water to kill him. But if you can do anything, feel [splagchnizomai toward] us and help us." (Mark 9:22)

"When [Jesus] he saw the crowds, he felt [splagchnizomai toward] them, because they were harassed and helpless, like sheep without a shepherd." (Matt 9:36)

"Filled with [splagchnizomai], Jesus reached out his hand and touched the man. "I am willing," he said. "Be clean!"" (Mark 1:41)

"So he got up and went to his father. But while he was still a long way off, his father saw him and was filled with [splagchnizomai] for him; he ran to his son, threw his arms around him and kissed him." (Luke 15:20)

Take heart

Three Morals of the Parable

1 The Foolish Servant is _____ the King, nor will he or she ever be.

2 The Boneheaded servant can't release his fellow servant because his own emptiness is _____.

3 At any time, the Boneheaded Servant could _____ to the Magnanimous King and ask to _____ with the fullness from the King.

Thoughts?:

"Remain in me, and I will remain in you. No branch can bear fruit by itself; it must remain in the vine. Neither can you bear fruit unless you remain in me. I am the vine; you are the branches. If a man remains in me and I in him, he will bear much fruit; apart from me you can do nothing" (John 15:4-13)

Forgiving Your Neighbor Spectrum (per Gal 5:6)

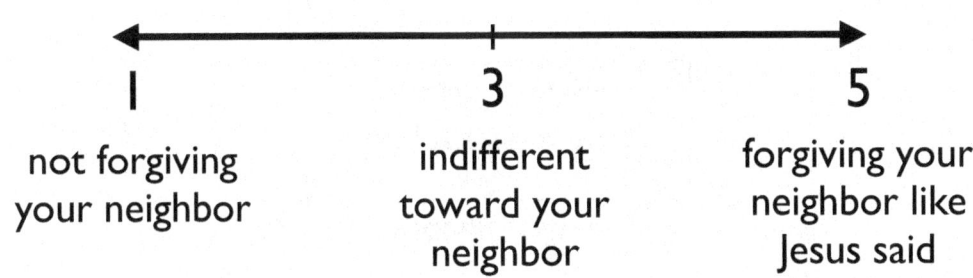

1 — not forgiving your neighbor

3 — indifferent toward your neighbor

5 — forgiving your neighbor like Jesus said

Thoughts:

Take heart

"Whether you do the right thing, or the wrong thing, neither end of the spectrum actually works—not really. Faith (a powerful "difference maker" from the Spirit) though makes love happen—or we could say, faith makes forgiveness happen—or the motivation to set others free from their debt to us happens." (Gal 5:6 revised)

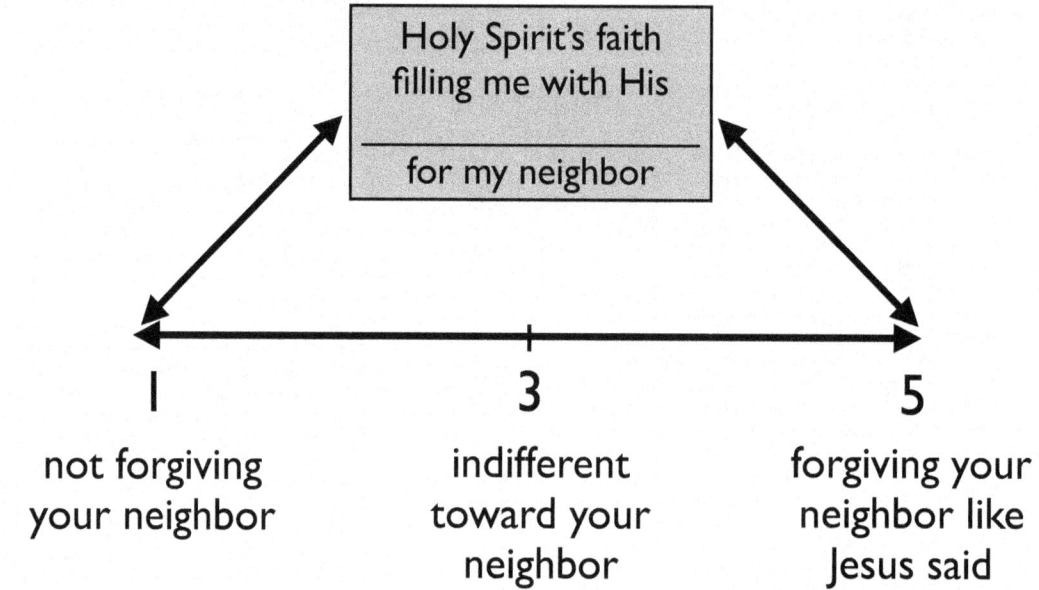

Thoughts:

"You bonehead, run to the always overflowing magnanimous King who loves you as much in your incompetence, irresponsible behavior, bad ethics, destructive ways of dealing with others, in your anger and rage, shame and guilt, fears and dysfunctions and ask to be made full! The minute amount that was owed to you by your fellow servant is not going to fill you. Period. If you want to be filled, you must go to a source that is larger than yourself. Full vessels act differently. Feel differently. Filling is what the Magnanimous King does. Run to the spring of living water of His splagchnizomai. You can't forgive without it. With the King's splag, you will notice a difference how you respond to others. You will feel it."

(from Take Heart: Sequel Module 4 video)

The Forgiving Path

The Forgiving Path is a web-based forgiveness intervention experience. Any Jesus-Follower can bring any crime, wounding, hurt, or disrespect that he or she just has not found relief for--has not been able to forgive.

It is very Biblical, confidential, anonymous, and very powerful. It takes about 90 minutes to complete. You can do it from anywhere, any time, as long as you have an internet connection.

Does it work? The amount of scientific changes as a result of only 90 minutes were stunning. Based upon analysis of the scientific before-and-after self-assessment surveys, the 400 regular people, some with horrific stories of injustice and abuse on average reported the following results:

27% reduction in desire to avoid the perpetrator

25% reduction in desire for revenge

40% increase in benevolence for the person who hurt me

96% increase in experience of justice for the crime

Remember, this was after only 90 minutes at the interactive nine stations. These are dramatic changes for only 90 minutes. Not perfect of course, that would be Heaven. But nonetheless, the changes should be noticeable.

There is a minimal fee to go through the Forgiving Path, but it is only a fraction of a single counseling visit. Check out http://fairforgiveness.com/is-forgiving-path-for-you/ to evaulate if the Forgiving Path is for you.

Check out http://fairforgiveness.com/is-forgiving-path-for-you/

Preaching the Gospel to Myself

" God, so how am I supposed to forgive seventy times seven times? Right now, I don't want to. It's still not fair, or right, or just. What about me? My loss? My scars? I can't. I see that now. Now I get the heavenly joke. Unless I am regularly filled with the DNA of the King, Your DNA, by faith, through the Holy Spirit in my inner-being, I will never be able to come anywhere near forgiving the crime committed against me. Not even close. My cup does not have the capacity. And it leaks. Whether I want to admit it or not, I am far more like the boneheaded servant than the ever-full magnanimous King. I desperately need You to make me feel the single absolute forgiveness that Jesus gained for me 2000 years ago. Then make me want to forgive. Give me some of your splagchnizomai, quick. Until that miracle occurs, I certainly am not free. Amen. "

Summary of Take Heart Sequel Week 4

1 I can't forgive, not on my own. My cup is too empty and I lack splagchnizomai which comes from God alone.

2 God is my only source for both of the things that I lack: fullness (Eph 3:14-21), justice, consolation, and splagchnizomai. All I need is need. All I need to do is to ask the Holy Spirit to give me both now.

3 The fruit of both fullness and splagchnizomai in me should be noticeable to myself and to others.

"REPENT therefore, and turn back, that your sins may be blotted out."
(Acts 3:19)

"Bear fruits in keeping with REPENTANCE. And do not begin to say to yourselves, 'We have Abraham as our father.' For I tell you, God is able from these stones to raise up children for Abraham. Even now the axe is laid to the root of the trees. Every tree therefore that does not bear good fruit is cut down and thrown into the fire."
(Luke 3:8-9)

"Therefore, O King Agrippa, I was not disobedient to the heavenly vision, but declared first to those in Damascus, then in Jerusalem and throughout all the region of Judea, and also to the Gentiles, that they should REPENT and turn to God, performing deeds in keeping with their REPENTANCE."
(Acts 26:19-20)

"The Lord is not slow to fulfill his promise as some count slowness, but is patient toward you, not wishing that any should perish, but that all should reach REPENTANCE." (2 Pet 3:9)

"Repentance is an internal shift in our perceived source of life It is recognizing that our self-protective means to avoiding hurt have not ushered us into real living (the reckless abandon to God that ultimately leads to a deep sense of wholeness and joy) or to purposeful, powerful relating. Repentance is the process of deeply acknowledging the supreme call to love, which is violated at every moment, in every relationship--a law that applies even to those who have been heinously victimized. The law of love removes excuses...Repentance involves the response of humble hunger, bold movement, and wild celebration when faced with the reality of our fallen state and the grace of God. The Father wants us to be hungry and dissatisfied with our pigpen cuisine. He wants us to return in absolute dependence and dine on the fatted calf. Repentance flows from the energy of being stunned, silent, and without excuse for the harm we've done to ourselves and others and for breaking the heart of God. It includes a hunger-based refusal to wallow in anything that makes us less human, strips anyone of his dignity, or damages our relationship with the Lord."
Dan Allendar

Module #5: Miraculous Repentance

"This is what the Sovereign LORD, the Holy One of Israel, says: 'In REPENTANCE and rest is your salvation, in quietness and trust is your strength, but you would have none of it.'" (Isa 30:15)

Your Preliminary Definition of Repentance

What is Repentance?

Write down a specific recent instance where you have struggled to really repent (Please use abbreviations to keep it anonymous).

take heart

Engaging Repentance: Psalm 51

1 Have mercy on me, O God, according to your unfailing love; according to your great compassion blot out my transgressions (Hebrew: pesha). 2 Wash away all my iniquity (Hebrew: avon) and cleanse me from my sin (Hebrew: chet). 3 For I know my transgressions, and my sin is always before me.

4 Against you, you only, have I sinned and done what is evil in your sight, so that you are proved right when you speak and justified when you judge.

5 Surely I was sinful at birth, sinful from the time my mother conceived me. 6 Surely you desire truth in the inner parts; you teach me wisdom in the inmost place. 7 Cleanse me with hyssop, and I will be clean; wash me, and I will be whiter than snow.

8 Let me hear joy and gladness; let the bones you have crushed rejoice. 9 Hide your face from my sins and blot out all my iniquity.

10 Create in me a pure heart, O God, and renew a steadfast spirit within me.

11 Do not cast me from your presence or take your Holy Spirit from me. 12 Restore to me the joy of your salvation and grant me a willing spirit, to sustain me."
Psalm 51:1-12

Notes:
"*transgressions...*"
Hebrew "pesha". Pesha implies that one acted in rebellion against the standard, against the law, authority, God or societal norms. There is "doing right" being pro-other, pro-community, pro-God and then there is pesha.

"*iniquity...*"
Hebrew "avon." Avon can refer to a deviation from, a bending, twisting or distortion of something that would cause harm or destruction to others.

"*sin...*"
Hebrew "chet." Chet means that he has "missed the mark." Think of chet as destructive, anti-social actions that give less than what is due or right to others. It is a failure to respect the full rights of others.

Adjust and update your definition of repentance?

A Closer Look at Sorrow and Repentance

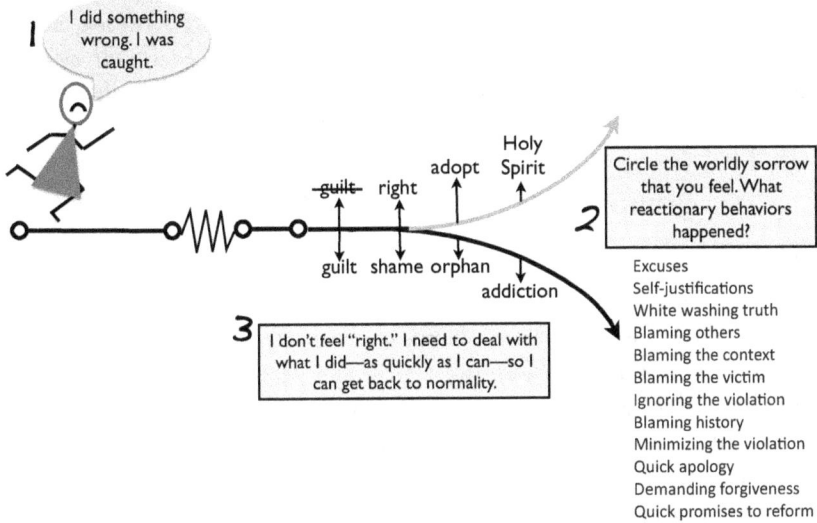

How familiar is this?
Humans cannot stand to not feel right or to not be seen as right by others. It creates stress which ignites stress-coping mechanisms. Here is a partial list of typical "worldly sorrow" coping strategies. Circle the one(s) that most closely align with your failed unsatisfying "repentance."

- Excuses ("I misunderstood what you meant."),
- Self-justifications ("I meant well, it just came out wrong."),
- Blaming others ("Look, my supervisor beat me up earlier and I was upset, OK?"),
- Whitewashing the history so that you look good ("That's not how I remember it...")
- Blaming the context ("Well I wouldn't have done it except that I was having a bad day and you just happened along," "I've been under stress lately; its not about you, its about my miserable life."),
- Blaming the victim ("You just should have said something."),
- Ignoring the violation ("Time heals all wounds."),
- Blaming history ("My father treated me the very same way. I guess I get it from him."),
- Minimizing the violation ("Well, I didn't mean to hurt you. That wasn't my intent." "Look it wasn't all that bad was it?"),
- Not accepting responsibility ("I am sorry if I hurt you."),
- Giving a quick apology just to get it over with ("Look, I am sorry, I really am, let's move on from here, OK?"),
- Demanding forgiveness ("I said I was sorry; the Christian thing would be to forgive me."),
- Issuing quick promises to reform ("I messed up, but I promise I'll never do it again.").

Take heart

Engage: Godly Sorrow Versus Worldly Sorrow

Remember the recent situation that you wrote down on the first page, where you admit that you hurt someone, did something to someone, said something about someone, committed some crime that you still feel guilt over even now? Now we can see that it is most helpful to portray it primarily as a crime against relationship (love God, love neighbor). Make sense?

en·gage groups Read 2 Corinthians 7:10-11 in your Engage groups and relate it to the specific situation with which you are dealing.

Background: The Corinthian church was a mess. It was hardly unified, it was divided up into a variety of theological and personality camps. It was harboring a wide variety of ethical and moral criminals, and the leadership, implicitly or explicitly, participated in cover-ups. Some even rejected Paul and his Apostolic credentials. From the top down, the church had problems. In First Corinthians, Paul blasted the church for their anti-Gospel, anti-God, and anti-community actions and choices. It seemed to work. In this next letter, Paul observes a dramatic miraculous change among them. Very observable. He notices the presence of Godly sorrow where before there was only self-righteousness, defensiveness, blaming, excuse making. Listen to Paul.

> "Godly sorrow brings repentance that leads to salvation and leaves no regret, but worldly sorrow brings death. See what this godly sorrow has produced in you: what earnestness, what eagerness to clear yourselves, what indignation, what alarm, what longing, what concern, what readiness to see justice done. At every point you have proved yourselves to be innocent in this matter." (2 Cor 7:10-11 NIV)

Eight (8) things that "Godly Sorrow" made happen in the heart of Corinthian Jesus-Followers

1) …a repentance that led to a fresh experience of their salvation.
2) …an earnestness (likely a seriousness to deal with all of the issues related to their actions and behaviors against God and Paul).
3) …a new motivation
4) …an indignation (likely at their crimes, how they hurt and offended Paul, at their flesh),
5) …a fear (likely fear of God),
6) …a longing (likely longing to be reconciled with Paul),
7) …a zeal (an intentional desire and motivation likely to be reconciled with Paul)
8) …a readiness to see justice done (perhaps related to the normal consequences of their crimes against Paul, or the slander of the enemies of Paul).

? Engage #1
Look at the list of things that Godly sorrow produced in the Corinthians and pick the one that just might make a difference in your situation? Please explain.

? Engage #2- (for the whole group)
Concisely put, what then is the difference between worldly and Godly sorrow? Adjust your definition of repentance if need be.

Six Pro-Relational Movements of Repentance

"So from now on we regard no one from a worldly point of view. Though we once regarded Christ in this way, we do so no longer. Therefore, if anyone is in Christ, he is a new creation; the old has gone, the new has come! All this is from God, who reconciled us to himself through Christ and gave us the ministry of reconciliation: that God was reconciling the world to himself in Christ, not counting men's sins against them. And he has committed to us the message of reconciliation. We are therefore Christ's ambassadors, as though God were making his appeal through us. We implore you on Christ's behalf: Be reconciled to God. God made him who had no sin to be sin for us, so that in him we might become the righteousness of God."

(2 Cor 5:16-21)

> **So what is repentance then?**
> Here is our shot at a first pass definition. Instead of seeing repentance as merely a new understanding (change of mind) regarding sin, or a change of direction, or the presence of sadness and empathy, its far more helpful to see repentance as the necessary fruit of our embracing godly sorrow—by faith through the Holy Spirit in us.

It is a start. To flesh it out a bit more, we would suggest that Biblical repentance involves, to one degree or another, six pro-relational movements that come from the Holy Spirit's DNA, not ours:

1. An awareness and sorrow over a relational breech that you caused by actions or inactions,
2. An admission of the latter with the implication of sorrow, compassion for victim(s), empathy, an understanding of the loss, the pain, the cost, the injustice involved (which implies a dialogue or investigation related to the victim),
3. The willingness to accept appropriate accountability for all known offenses and losses incurred,
4. A new willingness to embrace justice's demands (punishment, restitution, change in relational status),
5. A change of relational motivation toward the other,
6. A determination and stated intention to positively change future behavior so that trust can begin to be restored.

Not all repentances have all of the above elements in place 100% of the time.

Repentance is the result of an ongoing miracle of God accomplished through the Holy Spirit in us where we are beginning to see the relational breach that we caused, regret it, and are willing to move to pro-social reconciliation, to really want to heal the relational breaches in which we were admittedly causal through action or inaction.

What is the Difference Between "Godly" and "Worldly" Sorrow?

One comes from _____ and is accessed by faith, through the Holy Spirit in your inner being. The other doesn't!

One is about restored _____. The other is about soothing remorse, protecting reputation, and working hard to trying harder to do the right thing on your own juice.

Repentance Spectrum pre-Godly Sorrow (Gal 5:6)

"For in Christ Jesus whether you do the right thing, or choose to do the wrong thing, or nothing at all, none of those choices have the capability to accomplish anything. On the other hand, the only thing that really has the capability to come close to accomplish your deeper real goal is Faith, that is the Faith that comes from the Holy Spirit alone. It innately makes love happen. By the way, that includes you feeling love, and you feeling love for God and other people too." (Gal 5:6 revised)

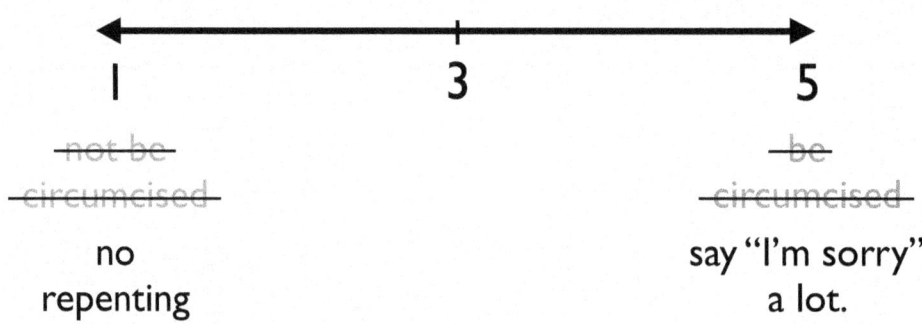

1	3	5
~~not be circumcised~~		~~be circumcised~~
no repenting		say "I'm sorry" a lot.

Repentance Spectrum post-Godly Sorrow (Gal 5:6)

"For in Christ Jesus whether you repent religiously all the time, or have stopped repenting at all—neither effort, or lack of effort has the capability to accomplish anything—at least not what you are hoping for. On the other hand, the only thing that really works—I mean really--is "faith", which you can't do—that Faith is a fruit of the Spirit, not some undiscovered atrophied muscle group in you, only the Faith of the Spirit unleashed in you can actually make you feel godly sorrow for what you have done and the breach in the relationship your actions or inactions have caused. That godly sorrow makes real repentance happen in your gut. That will definitely change how you repent and do works of repentance."

(Gal 5:6 revised to cover repentance)

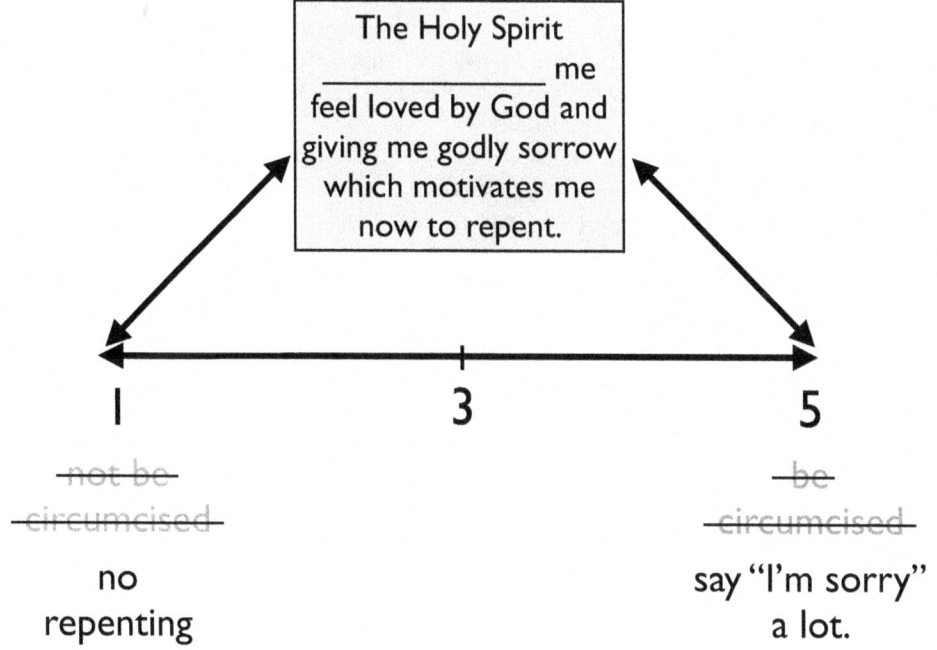

Preaching the Gospel to My Worldly Sorrow

Pair off. Have Person A say the Repentance Prayer #1 to Person B. Then Person B is invited to say Repentance Prayer #2 to Person A. Then switch. Take a deep breath and focus on being present and truly hearing what is being said.

Repentance Prayer #1

"God, I am tired of being in this situation. I know that it is not where You want me to be. I get that. I know that I am out of sync with You. So I need You, now. I can see that I messed up, that I hurt someone that I should have treated with love, kindness and respect. Sure, I feel bad about it. But I also feel that it's not all my fault. What about them? What about what they did? Surely there is plenty of blame to go around, right God? When are they going to apologize to me? I said I was sorry, and apparently that wasn't good enough. Now what?

OK, Wow, where did all of that worldly sorrow come from? Yuck. You are right again God. I can't seem to repent, not well. If I was really honest I would admit to You that I guess I am not that sorry, at least not with a godly sorrow. Nothing miraculous for sure. So I need something from You very quickly. First, right now, God make me feel how much You love me, in spite of my lack of repentance. Do You still love me as I am? You do? That's the Gospel? I need to hear it and feel it right now.

I need more of course. God, make me feel the sorrow that comes only from You, Your godly sorrow. Make me really feel the pain and damages that my actions, inactions and lack of caring for that person have caused to them and to our relationship. I am way out of sync with You and Your love for them. I need Your sorrow. Make me feel a new desire for a restored relationship with the person that I dissed. Make me feel the love You feel for them. I get it. Any resurrected relationship will take ongoing miracles from You. Such repentance is just not in me. Can I count on You for that, too? God, don't take the experience of Your Spirit away from Me."

Repentance Prayer #2

"May I share with you the same Gospel that I am preaching to myself? You likely need to be reminded how much God loves you right now, as you are not as you should be, whether you have truly repented or not. You cannot mess up your relationship with God, thank God. He will never take His Spirit from you, ever. That is such great news. With that in mind, let us both continue to struggle to access godly sorrow. Let's keep asking the Holy Spirit in us to make us feel authentic godly sorrow while at the same time looking up into the adoring eyes of our heavenly Father. No judgment. I hope this helps."

"Words fail to explain how necessary prayer is and in how many ways the exercise of prayer is profitable."
John Calvin

Module #6: Miraculous Prayer

"Prayer is the primary exercise of faith."
John Calvin

You do not have, because you do not ask God.
James 4:2 NIV

John Bunyan Prayer Quotes (from "On Prayer")

"Prayer opens the heart to God, and it is the means by which the soul, though empty, is filled with God."

"The best prayer I ever prayed had enough sin to damn the whole world."

"When thou prayest, rather let thy heart be without words, than thy words without a heart."

"It is not the mouth that is the main thing to be looked at in prayer, but whether the heart is so full of affection and earnestness in prayer with God, that it is impossible to express their sense and desire; for then a man desires indeed, when his desires are so strong, many, and mighty, that all the words, tears, and groans that can come from the heart, cannot utter them."

"The last thing that hindereth prayer is, the form of it without the power. It is an easy thing for men to be very hot for such things as forms of prayer, as they are written in a book; but yet they are altogether forgetful to inquire with themselves, whether they have the spirit and power of prayer. These men are like a painted man, and their prayers like a false voice. They in person appear as hypocrites, and their prayers are an abomination (Prov 28:9). When they say they have been pouring out their souls to God he saith they have been howling like dogs (Hos. 7:14)."

"Nothing but the Spirit can show a man clearly his misery by nature, and so put a man into a posture of prayer. Talk is but talk, as we use to say, and so it is but mouth-worship, if there be not a sense of misery, and that effectually too. O the cursed hypocrisy that is in most hearts, and that accompanieth many thousands of praying men that would be so looked upon in this day, and all for want of a sense of their misery! But now the Spirit, that will sweetly show the soul its misery, where it is, and what is like to become of it, also the intolerableness of that condition. For it is the Spirit that doth effectually convince of sin and misery, without the Lord Jesus, and so puts the soul into a sweet, sensible, affectionate way of praying to God according to his word (Jn. 16:7-9)."

How's Prayer Going for Me?

Consider each statement below and determine if you very much disagree with it, disagree, feel neutral, agree or very much agree. No right or wrong answer. Then add up your answers and analyze them based upon the score sheet below. (5 minutes)

	Very Much Disagree		Neutral		Very Much Agree
God is prone to bless those who really pray.	1	2	3	4	5
If Christians prayed more the Kingdom would grow faster.	1	2	3	4	5
I feel guilty if I forget to pray.	1	2	3	4	5
I feel shame when I consider my prayer life.	1	2	3	4	5
I pray but I am afraid that the heavens are very silent.	1	2	3	4	5
I know that God would like me more if I was more consistent in prayer.	1	2	3	4	5
I don't know what is wrong with me. I keep forgetting to pray when I know I should.	1	2	3	4	5
I go through seasons of consistent prayer and seasons of erratic prayer immersed in guilt.	1	2	3	4	5
I am jealous of those Christians who pray a lot. I have tried, but won't.	1	2	3	4	5
I have resolved that I am just not a prayer warrior.	1	2	3	4	5
Prayer is a painful topic. I am tired of hearing that I am a failure at it.	1	2	3	4	5
I feel guilty when I forget to pray and the bad thing happened.	1	2	3	4	5

Add up your scores from above. Compare it score sheet below.

Score 12-24: Healthy understanding of prayer
Score 25-35: Confusing understanding of prayer
Score 36-60: Unhealthy understanding of prayer

Possible Prayer Motivations

1 Are you praying to God, your Heavenly Father, because you feel right now how much He favors and loves you as you are?

or...

2 Are you praying so that you would get God's favor and love for you more?

Thoughts?:

Bible Study: Luke 18:9-14

"9 To some who were confident of their own righteousness and looked down on everyone else, Jesus told this parable:

10 "Two men went up to the temple to pray, one a Pharisee and the other a tax collector. 11 The Pharisee stood by himself and prayed: 'God, I thank you that I am not like other people—robbers, evildoers, adulterers—or even like this tax collector. 12 I fast twice a week and give a tenth of all I get.'

13 "But the tax collector stood at a distance. He would not even look up to heaven, but beat his breast and said, 'God, have mercy on me, a sinner.'

14 "I tell you that this man, rather than the other, went home justified before God. For all those who exalt themselves will be humbled, and those who humble themselves will be exalted."

(Luke 18:9-14 NIV)

Notes:

"have mercy..."
Greek "hilaskomai." Could be either mercy, make atonement for me, or forgive me, the result of which would be a restored relationship and reconciliation.

"justified..."
Made to be or proclaimed to be right with God.

"exalt themselves..."
Greek "hupsoo." To consider yourself better than others, or to despise others.

"humble themselves..."
Greek "taipenoo." One who causes his heart to bow down or even one who makes his heart small.

Engage Groups

Break up into your Engage groups and process the parable. Remember, everyone will have up to one minute to share their thoughts. There is to be no criticism of others, or debate, or argumentation. Not here, please. The Engage questions are meant to be provocative and so there are definitely more than one way to answer them legitimately. Cool? Your answers are honored here.

1 What made one prayer dramatically different than the other?

2 What were the different motivations that drove the two men to come into the presence of God to pray?

3 If someone was listening to your prayers today, where on the spectrum below would they put your prayers and motivation to pray?

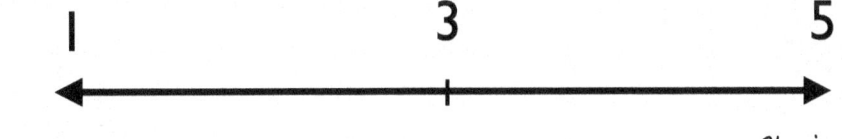

Tax Collector
Needy, religious failure, humble, laser-focused wanting to feel God's favor, lots of human reason to not think that God would ever listen.

Pharisee
Righteous, expectant that God will bless him/her based upon his/her efforts. Despises those "others" who do not live up to God's standards. Believes that he/she and God are good, but that couldn't be further from the truth.

4 According to Jesus, which one got what they wanted from their audience with God? What did they get?

Take heart

Galatians 5:6 Prayer Spectrum (before)

"For in Christ Jesus whether you do the right thing, or choose to do the wrong thing, or nothing at all, none of those choices have the capability to accomplish anything. On the other hand, the only thing that really has the capability to come close to accomplish your deeper real goal is Faith, that is, the "Faith" that comes from the Holy Spirit alone. This "Faith" innately makes love happen. By the way, that includes you feeling loved, and you feeling love for God and other people too."

Gal 5:6 (revised)

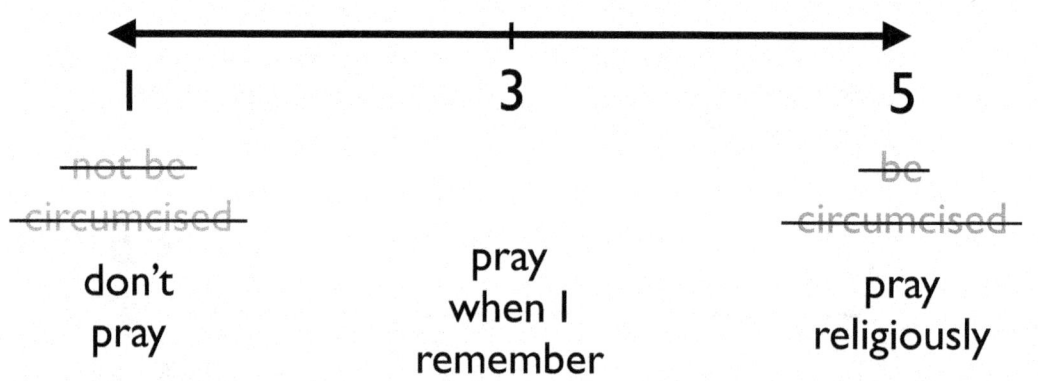

1 — don't pray ~~not be circumcised~~

3 — pray when I remember

5 — pray religiously ~~be circumcised~~

Galatians 5:6 Prayer Spectrum (after)

"For in Christ Jesus whether you pray religiously all the time, or have stopped praying at all—neither effort, or lack of effort has the capability to accomplish anything—at least not what you are hoping for. On the other hand, the only thing that really works—I mean really—is "faith", which you can't do—the faith that I speak of is the "Faith" which is a fruit of the Spirit, not some undiscovered atrophied muscle group in you. Only the "Faith" of the Spirit unleashed in you can actually make love for God, or others, happen in you. That will definitely change how you pray, why you pray, and what you pray."

Gal 5:6 (revised for prayer)

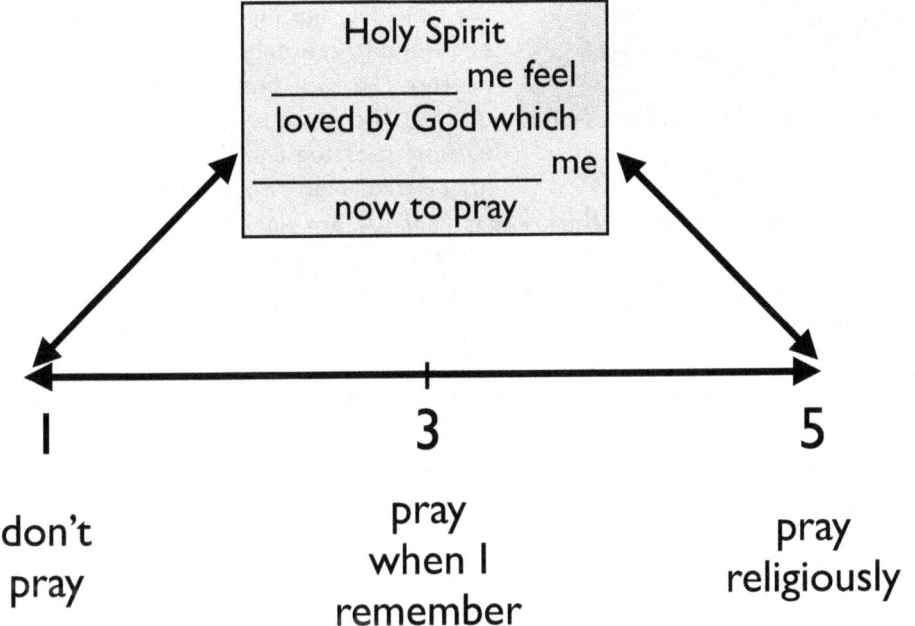

"How do you change your prayer life struggles? Ironically, you are invited to pray—but a specific prayer, all the time, and often. "God, before I bring all of my other stuff to you, make me feel your love for me right now." That is your first prayer, your second prayer, and maybe even your third prayer.
This alone will change how you approach your other more typical prayers.

(from Take Heart: Sequel, Module 5: Miraculous Prayer video)

take heart

Martin Luther's Posture of the Ground Prayer

"Here is a helpful image. Wouldn't it be absurd and enormous hubris for the thirsty dry ground to even think about demanding rain from the clouds? Picture the ground holding up its empty dry and cracked hands skyward believing that if it only did it right, held its hands up at 10 and 2 o'clock or 11 and 1 o'clock—or better waved them up and down frantically in some liturgical exercise believing that if it only did it right, the clouds would open up in a torrent of life-giving rain. No, hardly. The ground knows its place and humbly can only hold-up empty dry hands to receive the rain that God ordains to fall upon it. It is the same with righteousness. There is nothing that we can do that moves God to shift his original plan to rain righteousness down upon us. We must get it into our thick heads that we are not able to do anything by our own strength and works to win this heavenly and eternal righteousness; and therefore we shall never be able to get it, unless God Himself by mere imputation and by his unspeakable gift gives it to us."

(paraphrased from Luther's Preface to his Commentary on Galatians)

Thoughts:

Preaching the Gospel to Myself

> God, I am still pretty messed up. I have been struggling to pray for years and haven't moved forward much at all. I have been feeling that I was doing something wrong or not doing something right. Honestly, my prayer life has been a source of shame and guilt to me. But now I am beginning to get why. I now choose to stop doing prayer the way I was doing it. I had developed some bad habits. I forgot, first things first. So I am here now, like Luther's dry cracked ground, holding up empty and needy hands, palms-up, to receive from You everything that Jesus has already bought for me. God fill me with Faith through Christ's Spirit in me. Make me feel how much You really love me, like me, adore me, as I am, not as I should be or could be. Now please. My other prayers are still important, some very critical to my well-being, at least I think so. But, first things first. Abba, make me feel your love for me now. Amen.

Summary of Take Heart Week 5

1 I can't pray, not on my own. Too often I am praying do get God to pay attention, to like me again. All too quickly, I forget the Gospel.

2 First things first. My first prayer is to ask God to make me believe how much He really does love me right now, as I am, not as I should be.

3 Once I begin to embrace the height, width, length and depth of the love of God for me right now, my prayer life will dramatically and noticeable shift—most likely be more other oriented, more thankful, more free.

The Simple Uncluttered Gospel
Jesus-Follower, strictly because of what Jesus did for you 2000 years ago, God loves you as much as the Father loves the Son and the Son loves the Father, as you are, not as you should be or could be. You can't add to it or take away from it. I get it that is doesn't always feel like it. But you can take Biblical baby-steps to experience the love of God for you more—not perfectly, that is Heaven—but noticeably more than you do right now. That should make an observable difference in your sense of significance, security and belonging. How do you begin? Right now, ask the Spirit in you to make you feel His love for you and for others right now. Repeat that prayer again and again until a new habit starts to form. Then keep on saying that prayer every day, twice a day until you die.

(Eph 3:14-21, Rom 5:6-8, 1 Cor 13:4-8, John 13:34-35, Titus 2:11-13)

7 Module #7: Miraculous Evangelism

> "Therefore go and make disciples of all nations, baptizing them in the name of the Father and of the Son and of the Holy Spirit, and teaching them to obey everything I have commanded you. And surely I am with you always, to the very end of the age."
> (Matt 28:19-20 NIV)

Take Heart Sequel Review

Modules 1&2

Jesus Follower, strictly because of what Jesus did for you 2000 years ago, God can't _____ you again, or even be _____ ever!

God must/does _____ you!

You are perfectly _____ into the most amazing and loving relationship!

Module 3

You and I can't _____ others, not really!

Module 4

You and I can't _____, not on our own!

Module 5

You and I can't _____, not on our own!

Module 6

You and I can't even really _____, not by our own will and power!

Q: Wait a minute, are you saying that God commands us to do something that we can't do without His Spirit's power and help?

A: Do you mean like "Be perfect, even as your heavenly Father is perfect"? Or "Husbands, love your wives like Christ loves the church"? How about, "Go and sin no more"? Not to mention, "Forgive 70 times 7 times". Or "Love your enemy". Want more examples?

take heart

Pre-Evangelism Tips: Things You Need to Know

1 Jesus-Follower, God loves you, as you are, whether you _____ or not.

2 The two main hindrances to evangelism is
1) We are _____ of messing up.
   and,
2) We don't really _____ our neighbors.

Notes:

What Have We Begin To Learn About Our Neighbors?

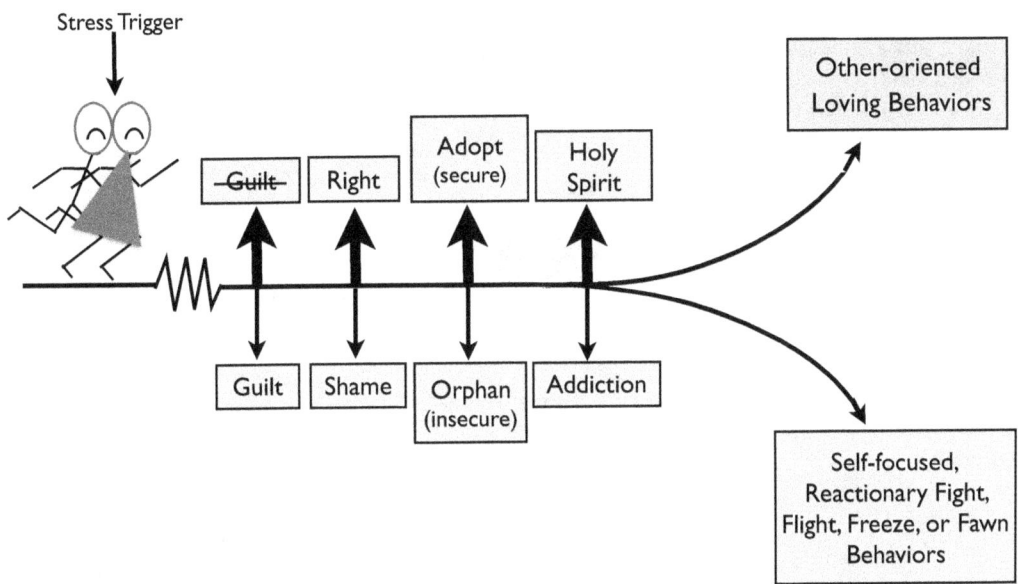

Notes:

Keep preaching the Simple Uncluttered Gospel to yourself every day. It will make a noticeable difference (Rom 1:16). You will begin to feel just a little bit more love for your neighbor.

The Simple Uncluttered Gospel

"Jesus-Follower, strictly because of what Jesus did for you 2000 years ago, God has to love you, He does love you with all of His heart, as much as the Father loves the Son and the Son loves the Father. He can't love you any more or any less than He does right now. He loves you as you are, not as you should be or could be. You can't add to this love, or take away from it. Now I get it, it often feels like you've messed it up, or need to do something so that God would like you better. Not so. Good news, there is something that you can do, and are invited to do. You can take daily baby-steps to ask the Spirit inside you to make you know, experience, feel, just how much God loves you right now. Also ask the Spirit to give you His love for your neighbor. Just ask. Ask again later today. Ask tomorrow. Make it a spiritual habit."

Bible Study: Philippians 2:1-5 NIV

1 If you have any encouragement from being united with Christ, if any comfort from his love, if any fellowship with the Spirit, if any tenderness and compassion,

2 then make my joy complete by being like-minded, having the same love, being one in spirit and purpose.

3 Do nothing out of selfish ambition or vain conceit, but in humility consider others better than yourselves.

4 Each of you should look not only to your own interests, but also to the interests of others.

5 Your attitude should be the same as that of Christ Jesus…".

(Phil 2:1-5 NIV)

Notes:

"fellowship…"
Gr. koinonia: Can refer to regular fellowship, friendship, or community, but in this context, Paul is likely speaking about a higher fellowship of the Spirit—the stuff of community that uniquely exists between God the Father, Son and Holy Spirit, that we can experience only through the Holy Spirit in us.

"tenderness…"
Gr. splagchnizomai: a deep-set positive other-oriented gut reaction when seeing hurting, oppressed, enslaved, dissatisfied people that motivates one to set people free. Innate to God. See page 45.

"in humility…"
Gr. taipenophrosune: The capacity to not take your own rights so seriously.

Unpacking Philippians 2:1-5 for Modern Audience

If you are experiencing outrageous encouragement right now, it is most likely because you are in Christ,

If you are experiencing the significance, security, and belonging that comes from the height, width, length and depth of God's love right now, it is because Jesus bought it for you,

If you are experiencing koinonia, the alien Holy Spirit-empowered love for others-over-self right now, it is His fingerprint, not yours.

If you are experiencing splagchnizomai, God's gut wrenching love for "others," those whom He loves as much as He loves you, this same splagchnizomai which necessarily drives Him to intervene to rescue, to set free, to bless right now, is now also motivating you too to want to go do something sacrificial for that person,

If you are experiencing new and unprecedented concern for those in your life who are suffering some painful misfortune, dissatisfaction, discontent, or who are acting like functional underachievers (compared to their vast potential) right now, be encouraged. This concern for others is the inevitable fruit of the Holy Spirit in you and through you.

Then Paul says, "Now make me really happy. Let's have some fun."

modified from the Take Heart: Sequel Module 7

Notes:

take heart

Galatians 5:6 Evangelism Spectrum (before)

"For in Christ Jesus whether you do the right thing, or choose to do the wrong thing, or nothing at all, none of those choices have the capability to accomplish anything. On the other hand, the only thing that really has the capability to come close to accomplish your deeper real goal is Faith, that is, the "Faith" that comes from the Holy Spirit alone. This "Faith" innately makes love happen. By the way, that includes you feeling loved, and you feeling love for God and other people too."

Gal 5:6 (revised)

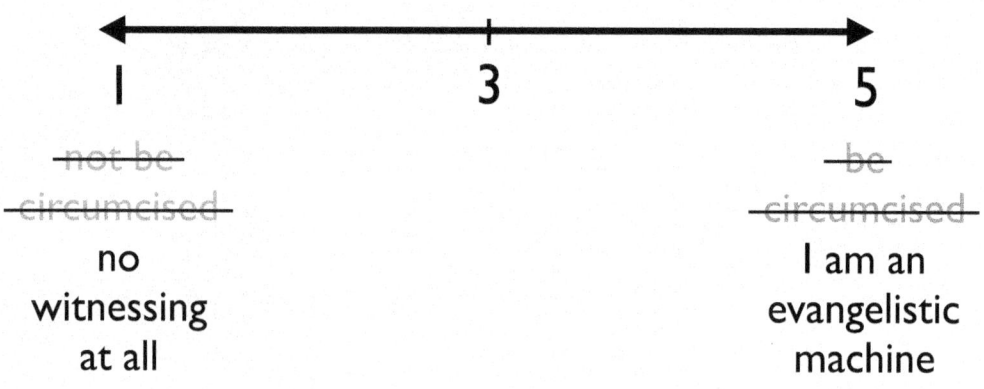

1 — ~~not be circumcised~~ — no witnessing at all

3

5 — ~~be circumcised~~ — I am an evangelistic machine

Galatians 5:6 Evangelism Spectrum (after)

"For in Christ Jesus whether you evangelize religiously all the time, or have stopped evangelizing at all—neither effort, or lack of effort has the capability to accomplish anything—at least not what you are hoping for. On the other hand, the only thing that really works—I mean really--is "faith", which you can't do—that Faith is a fruit of the Spirit, not some undiscovered atrophied muscle group in you, only the Faith of the Spirit unleashed in you can actually make love for God, or others happen in you. When you get how much God loves you, you will also feel more love for others (and so will want to sacrifice for them) and will feel less fear of falling flat on your face (perfect love casts out fear). That will definitely change how you evangelize, why you evangelize, and what you say as the good news." Gal 5:6 (revised for prayer)

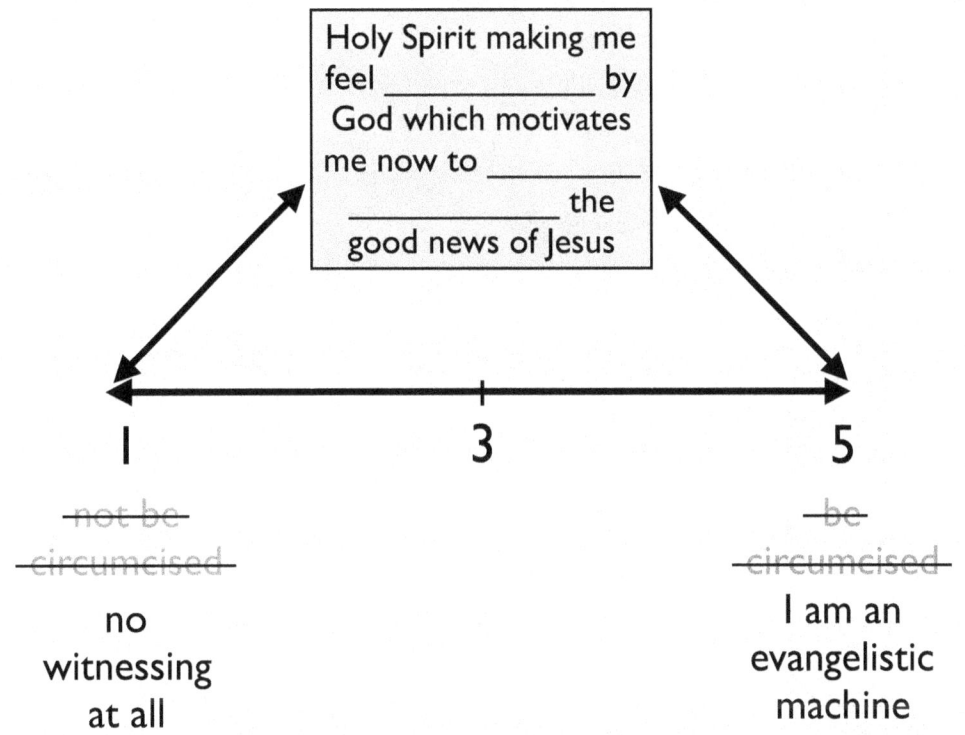

1 — no witnessing at all ~~not be circumcised~~

3

5 — I am an evangelistic machine ~~be circumcised~~

Holy Spirit making me feel _____ by God which motivates me now to _____ _____ the good news of Jesus

"This awareness is the core working of the Holy Spirit. It turns out that this is His passion for you. This alien love will change your day, change how you treat others. My guess is that if you get this, your evangelism will be transformed. You will begin to want to tell others the good news of Jesus. It will feel different—not a burden, not as scary, rather evangelism will become a personal relational exercise that you want to do more than anything else—not because you have to at all."

(from Take Heart: Sequel, Module 7: Miraculous Evangelism video)

Take heart

The Philippians 2 Survey

Consider each statement below and determine if you very much disagree with it, disagree, feel neutral, agree or very much agree. No right or wrong answer. Then add up your answers and analyze them based upon the score sheet below. (5 minutes)

	Strongly Disagree		Neutral		Strongly Agree
I am feeling surprising encouragement because of the Gospel right now.	1	2	3	4	5
I am really experiencing God's love for me right now, as I am.	1	2	3	4	5
I am thinking of my own rights less.	1	2	3	4	5
Others are observing that I am exhibiting a strange new concern for those who are suffering misfortune.	1	2	3	4	5
I am really feeling more other-oriented than self-oriented today.	1	2	3	4	5
I am experiencing a brand new noticeable deep concern for others who are beat-up, lost, depressed, broken, those who have been or are being treated with injustice, bigotry or abuse.	1	2	3	4	5
I am beginning to think of the needs of others more than I think of my own needs.	1	2	3	4	5

Add up your scores from above. Compare it score sheet below.
  Score 7-14: You are trying to do "Christianity" too much on your own.
  Score 15-24: Hit or miss experience of the Spirit in you.
  Score 25-35: Dance child of God, dance. Go and tell others what you are experiencing.

Preaching the Gospel to Myself

> God, I admit that it would appear that very few people have run to You because of my words or life testimony. I have tried to witness. I have not had the results that I had hoped for. I am discouraged, afraid of messing up, saying the wrong thing, or not saying the right thing. Is it true that I have been largely doing this on my own? Is it true that You have, all along, been ready to give me the desire of Jesus to tell others, the motivation of Jesus to rescue the lost, the heart of Jesus to actually love enemies? All I need to do is ask, daily? OK God, make me feel Your love for me, and for my friends and family. Make me feel Your concern for the lostness of my friends and family. Make me see them as You see them. Make me want to say to You, "Not my will be done, but Yours." Give me the desire, the love, and the words that can set them free. Now Father. Amen.

Take heart

"Preaching the Gospel to Myself" Review

Module #1: Miraculous Faith

> God, I am feeling a little bit hopeful about this, more than I have been about anything religious recently. This is giving me new hope that I can feel Your love now. I confess that Jesus purchased that love for me. I have tried working harder—doing more good things—studying to learn what the Bible says—trying harder to believe more but received very little fruit from that related to You and me, me and You. Other times, I just gave up—quit. What was the point, I thought? OK, I am here, I am in the posture of receiving from you, not doing anything to earn, to manipulate, to cajole—my hands are open and upward. Holy Spirit give me your power to know how much You love me as I am, not as I should be. Holy Spirit, now please, give me Your faith, to really, really know that I am in the heavenly number, a person in good standing, no probation, no unfinished tasks ahead of me, loved by You with all of the love in the universe, in spite of my lack of experience of that lately, from You or others. I wait. Quickly please. I struggle so much now.

Module #2: The Simple Unlcuttered Gospel

> God, I am feeling a little bit more hopeful about this, more than I have been about anything religious recently. This is giving me new hope that I can feel Your love now. I confess that Jesus purchased that love for me. I have tried working harder—doing more good things—studying to learn what the Bible says—trying harder to believe more but received very little fruit from that related to You and me, me and You. Other times, I just gave up—quit. What was the point, I thought? OK, I am here, I am in the posture of receiving from you, not doing anything to earn, to manipulate, to cajole—my hands are open and upward. Holy Spirit give me your power to know how much You love me as I am, not as I should be. Holy Spirit, now please, give me Your faith, to really, really know that I am in the heavenly number, a person in good standing, no probation, no unfinished tasks ahead of me, loved by You with all of the love in the universe, in spite of my lack of experience of that lately from You or others here. I wait. Quickly please. I struggle so much now.

Module #3: Miraculous Relationships

> God, right now I am hurting, depressed, angry, feeling disrespected, unloved, hopeless, beat-up, ashamed and feel like a failure…and that's just the tip of the iceberg. I really don't like this person. I wish I never knew them. To some degree, I despise them. I am also afraid of them. I can't take it being with them, being near them anymore. My body has a visceral reaction when I am in the same room. Honestly, I am at the end of my rope. I admit that You love them as they are, even after all the things they did to me, the many things they didn't do for me. I don't. I confess that I am way out of sync with You—in fact, this frightens me. Honestly, I am afraid that You can make me love them again. I am not sure at all that I want that to happen. I am done. However, I am willing to come to You to ask that You make me feel loved by You again. I need that. I want that desperately. Holy Spirit, unleash Your faith in my inner-being and make love happen for me. Now please. Amen.
>
> {addendum for when you are ready}
>
> I am also begging that You give me Your love for them. This is hard right now. I am not so sure that I really want it. This is pretty scary. So give me Your perfect love that casts out fears. Give me wisdom so I don't go and do something stupid. Amen.

Module #4: Miraculous Forgiving

> God, so how am I supposed to forgive seventy times seven times? Right now, I don't want to. It's still not fair, or right, or just. What about me? My loss? My scars? I can't. I see that now. Now I get the heavenly joke. Unless I am regularly filled with the DNA of the King, Your DNA, by faith, through the Holy Spirit in my inner-being, I will never be able to come anywhere near forgiving the crime committed against me. Not even close. My cup does not have the capacity. And it leaks. Whether I want to admit it or not, I am far more like the boneheaded servant than the ever-full magnanimous King. I desperately need You to make me feel the single absolute forgiveness that Jesus gained for me 2000 years ago. Then make me want to forgive. Give me some of your splagchnizomai, quick. Until that miracle occurs, I certainly am not free. Amen.

Module #5: Miraculous Repentance

> God, I am tired of being in this situation. I know that it is not where You want me to be. I get that. I know that I am out of sync with You. So I need You, now. I can see that I messed up, that I hurt someone that I should have treated with love, kindness and respect. Sure, I feel bad about it. But I also feel that it's not all my fault. What about them? What about what they did? Surely there is plenty of blame to go around, right God? When are they going to apologize to me? I said I was sorry, and apparently that wasn't good enough. Now what?
>
> OK, Wow, where did all of that worldly sorrow come from? Yuck. You are right again God. I can't seem to repent, not well. If I was really honest I would admit to You that I guess I am not that sorry, at least not with a godly sorrow. Nothing miraculous for sure. So I need something from You very quickly. First, right now, God make me feel how much You love me, in spite of my lack of repentance. Do You still love me as I am? You do? That's the Gospel? I need to hear it and feel it right now.
>
> I need more of course. God, make me feel the sorrow that comes only from You, Your godly sorrow. Make me really feel the pain and damages that my actions, inactions and lack of caring for that person have caused to them and to our relationship. I am way out of sync with You and Your love for them. I need Your sorrow. Make me feel a new desire for a restored relationship with the person that I dissed. Make me feel the love You feel for them. I get it. Any resurrected relationship will take ongoing miracles from You, Such repentance is just not in me. Can I count on You for that too? God, don't take the experience of Your Spirit away from Me.

Module #6: Miraculous Prayer

> God, I am still pretty messed up. I have been struggling to pray for years and haven't moved forward much at all. I have been feeling that I was doing something wrong or not doing something right. Honestly, my prayer life has been a source of shame and guilt to me. But now I am beginning to get why. I now choose to stop doing prayer the way I was doing it. I had developed some bad habits. I forgot, first things first. So I am here now, like Luther's dry cracked ground, holding up empty and needy hands, palms-up, to receive from You everything that Jesus has already bought for me. God fill me with Faith through Christ's Spirit in me. Make me feel how much You really love me, like me, adore me, as I am, not as I should be or could be. Now please. My other prayers are still important, some very critical to my well-being, at least I think so. But, first things first. Abba, make me feel your love for me now. Amen.

.

Module #7: Miraculous Evangelism

> God, I admit that it would appear that very few people have run to You because of my words or life testimony. I have tried to witness. I have not had the results that I had hoped for. I am discouraged, afraid of messing up, saying the wrong thing, or not saying the right thing. Is it true that I have been largely doing this on my own? Is it true that You have, all along, been ready to give me the desire of Jesus to tell others, the motivation of Jesus to rescue the lost, the heart of Jesus to actually love enemies? All I need to do is ask, daily? OK God, make me feel Your love for me, and for my friends and family. Make me feel Your concern for the lostness of my friends and family. Make me see them as You see them. Make me want to say to You, "Not my will be done, but Yours." Give me the desire, the love, and the words that can set them free. Now Father. Amen.

Partial Bibliography

Allender, Dan B. *The Wounded Heart: Hope for Adult Victims of Childhood Sexual Abuse.* Colorado Springs, Co.: Nav Press, 1990.

Anderson, E. *Code of the Street: Decency, Violence, and the Moral Life of the Inner City.* W.W. Norton Company, 1999.

Brown, B. *I Thought It Was Just Me (but it isn't): Making the Journey from "What Will People Think?" to "I Am Enough".* Avery 2007.

Bunyan, J. *Prayer.* Banner of Truth, 1989.

Calvin, J. *Institutes of the Christian Religion*, 1536 Edition. Eerdmans Publishing Company, 1986.

Duhigg, C. *The Power of Habit: Why We Do What We Do in Life and Business.* Random House, 2014.

Forbes, Heather, and Bryan Post, *Beyond Consequences Logic and Control: A Love-Based Approach to Helping Children with Severe Behaviors.* Boulder, Co.:BCI, 2009.

Sinek, S. *Start with Why: How Great Leaders Inspire Everyone to Take Action.* Penguin Group US, 2009.

Johnson, S. with Sanderfer, K. *Created for Connection: The 'Hold Me Tight' Guide for Christian Couples.* Little, Brown and Company, 2016.

Keller, T. *Counterfeit Gods: The Empty Promises of Money, Sex, and Power, and the Only Hope That Matters.* Penguin Group, 2009.

Keller, T. *The Freedom of Self-Forgetfulness.* 10Publishing, 2012.

Lewis, C.S. *The Great Divorce: A Dream.* Harper San Francisco, 1946.

Lovelace, R. *Dynamics of Spiritual Life: An Evangelical Theology of Renewal.* Inter-Varsity Press, 1979.

Mandolfo, C. *Daughter Zion Talks Back to the Prophets: A Dialogic Theology of the Book of Lamentations.* SBL, 2007.

Manning, B. *The Furious Longing Of God.* David C. Cook, 2009.

Mate, Gabor, *In the Realm of Hungry Ghosts: Close Encounters with Addiction.* Knopf Canada, 2008.

Olley, J.W. "'Righteousness'-Some Issues in Old Testament Translation Into English," *The Bible Translator 38*(3) (July 1987): 307-315.

Peterson, E. *The Message: The Bible in Contemporary Language.* NavPress, 2010.

Powlison, D. "Idols of the Heart and 'Vanity Fair'" posted Oct 16, 2009. http://www.ccef.org/idols-heart-and-vanity-fair.

Senyard, B. *Fair Forgiveness: Finding the Power to Forgive, Where You Least Expect It*. LE Press, 2014.
---- *The Gospel App Shape*. LE Press, 2015
---- *The Kiss of God: Rediscovering the Song of Songs*. LE Press, 2010.

Tell, B. *Lay It Down: Living in the Freedom of the Gospel*. NavPress, 2015.

Thompson, C. *The Soul of Shame" Retelling the Stories We Believe About Ourselves*. IVP Books, 2015.

www.ingramcontent.com/pod-product-compliance
Lightning Source LLC
Chambersburg PA
CBHW080600090426
42735CB00016B/3297